Go Programming for Beginners, Learn Go and Build Real-World Applications

A Beginner's Guide to Mastering Go Language and Crafting Efficient Software

Booker Blunt

Rafael Sanders

Miguel Farmer

Boozman Richard

Contents

How to Scan a Barcode to Get a Repository

1. **Install a QR/Barcode Scanner** – Ensure you have a barcode or QR code scanner app installed on your smartphone or use a built-in scanner in **GitHub, GitLab, or Bitbucket.**

2. **Open the Scanner** – Launch the scanner app and grant necessary camera permissions.

3. **Scan the Barcode** – Align the barcode within the scanning frame. The scanner will automatically detect and process it.

4. **Follow the Link** – The scanned result will display a **URL to the repository.** Tap the link to open it in your web browser or Git client.

5. **Clone the Repository** – Use **Git clone** with the provided URL to download the repository to your local machine.

Chapter 1: Getting Started with Go

1. Introduction

In today's fast-paced world of software development, choosing the right programming language can be the difference between a successful project and one that struggles to keep up with evolving requirements. **Go,** also known as **Golang,** is emerging as one of the most robust and efficient languages for modern software engineering. Born out of the need for simplicity, performance, and scalable design, Go offers an ideal blend of simplicity and power that appeals to everyone—from the novice programmer writing their first line of code to the experienced developer building complex distributed systems.

This chapter aims to demystify Go, starting from the very basics. We begin by defining what Go is, delve into its history and evolution, and explore why so many developers and organizations are embracing it for everything from web development to microservices. Whether you are completely new to programming or have experience with other languages, this guide is designed to provide you with a solid foundation, along with practical examples and projects that you can build upon.

What Makes Go Special?

Go was designed with the philosophy of simplicity and efficiency at its core. Its syntax is clear, the language structure is straightforward, and the toolchain is powerful yet easy to use. Unlike many other languages that come with steep learning curves, Go provides a more intuitive path for getting work done—especially when it comes to concurrency and high-performance networking.

Imagine being able to build a highly scalable application without getting bogged down by the complexity of thread management or memory leaks. With Go's built-in support for concurrency through goroutines and channels, you can manage multiple operations in parallel without a great deal of overhead. This is one of the key reasons why many modern, high-performance applications are being built in Go.

Setting the Stage

Before diving into the technical details, it's important to understand some of the key concepts and terminology that you'll encounter throughout this chapter:

- **Compiled Language:** Go is a compiled language, meaning that the code you write is transformed into executable machine code by a compiler before it runs. This results in fast execution and efficient resource management.

- **Static Typing:** Variables in Go have a fixed type, which helps catch errors at compile time and enhances code clarity.

- **Concurrency:** Go's approach to concurrency is built directly into the language. Goroutines (lightweight threads) and channels (for communication between goroutines) simplify the process of writing concurrent code.

- **Simplicity and Readability:** One of the main design goals of Go is to keep the language simple and easy to read, reducing the cognitive load on developers and allowing them to focus on solving problems rather than wrestling with complex language features.

As you progress through this chapter, you'll see these concepts come to life with practical examples and hands-on projects. Our goal is to ensure that you not only understand how Go works but also feel confident in using it to build real-world applications.

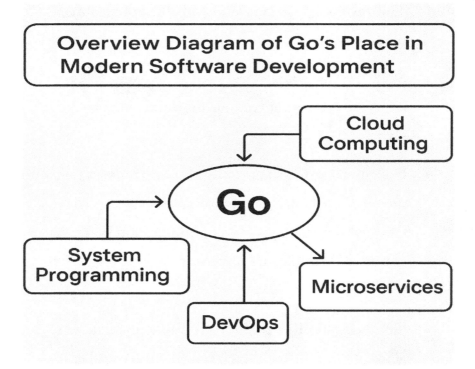

By the end of this chapter, you'll have set up your own Go development environment, written your first "Hello, World!" program, and gained insights into why Go is a language worth investing in. Let's begin our journey into the world of Go programming by exploring its origins and evolution.

---

2. Core Concepts and Theory

In this section, we delve into the core concepts that define the Go programming language. We'll cover the following topics in detail:

- **What is Go?**

- **History and Evolution**

- **Why Choose Go for Modern Software Development?**

2.1 What Is Go?

Go, often referred to as Golang because of its domain name (golang.org), is an open-source programming language developed by Google. It was created to address some of the inherent challenges in building large-scale, high-performance applications, particularly in areas like concurrent computing and networked services.

Key Features of Go:

- **Simplicity:** Go was designed to have a minimalistic syntax. There are no extraneous keywords or overly complex structures, making it easier for developers to write and maintain code.

- **Performance:** Since Go is a compiled language, its performance is comparable to that of C or C++. The efficiency of Go's runtime and garbage collection system makes it suitable for building performance-critical applications.

- **Concurrency:** One of the crown jewels of Go is its support for concurrency. Goroutines allow multiple functions to run concurrently, and channels provide a safe way to communicate between these goroutines.

- **Tooling:** The Go ecosystem includes a powerful set of built-in tools for formatting code, managing dependencies, testing, and profiling performance. This all-in-one approach helps reduce the complexity often associated with software development.

Example: A Simple Go Program

Below is an example of a basic Go program that prints "Hello, World!" to the console:

```go
package main

import "fmt"

func main() {
    fmt.Println("Hello, World!")
}
```

Explanation:

- The package main declaration defines the entry point for the executable.

- The import "fmt" statement includes the standard formatting library.

- The main function is where the execution of the program begins, and fmt.Println outputs text to the console.

2.2 History and Evolution

Understanding the evolution of Go provides context for its design and functionality. Go was conceived by Robert Griesemer, Rob Pike, and Ken Thompson at Google in 2007 and officially announced in 2009. The language was born out of the need to handle the growing complexity of software systems at Google, where existing languages struggled to offer both performance and ease of use.

Milestones in Go's Development:

- **2007-2009:** Initial development and release of Go as an open-source language. The team aimed to create a language that combined the speed of C with the ease of programming in dynamic languages.

- **2012:** Go 1.0 was released, establishing a stable foundation for developers. This release marked the beginning of Go's journey as a production-ready language.

- **2015 and Beyond:** Continuous improvements have been made to the language and its toolchain. Go's ecosystem has expanded with a growing number of libraries, frameworks, and community contributions. Major releases have focused on enhancing performance, concurrency features, and overall developer experience.

Impact on the Industry:

Go's clean syntax and efficient performance have made it a popular choice in many domains, including cloud services, DevOps tools, and microservices. Companies like Dropbox, Uber, and Netflix have adopted Go for various performance-critical applications. This widespread adoption is a testament to Go's ability to handle modern software demands while keeping development simple and efficient.

2.3 Why Choose Go for Modern Software Development?

There are several compelling reasons why Go has become a favored language in the modern software development landscape:

1. **Performance and Efficiency:**

   Being a compiled language, Go produces fast and efficient binaries. Its garbage collection system is designed to minimize pauses and maximize throughput, which is essential for high-performance applications.

2. **Simplicity and Readability:**

   Go's syntax is intentionally simple, reducing the learning curve for beginners while making it easier for teams to read and maintain code. This simplicity also leads to fewer bugs and a more predictable development process.

3. **Built-In Concurrency:**

   In today's multi-core world, the ability to execute tasks concurrently is crucial. Go's goroutines and channels provide a lightweight and intuitive model for handling concurrency, making it easier to write scalable and responsive applications.

4. **Robust Standard Library:**

   Go comes with a comprehensive standard library that covers everything from string manipulation to networking. This built-in functionality means you can accomplish many tasks without the need for external libraries, ensuring consistency and reducing dependency issues.

5. **Strong Community and Ecosystem:**
The growth of Go's community means a wealth of resources is available—tutorials, open-source projects, and professional support. Whether you're troubleshooting an issue or looking for best practices, you can tap into a global network of developers.

6. **Ideal for Microservices:**
Go's simplicity, performance, and built-in support for concurrency make it an excellent choice for microservices architecture. Its small binaries and ease of deployment are particularly attractive in cloud environments and containerized applications.

Real-World Analogy:
Imagine building a house with prefabricated components that are designed to fit together seamlessly. Go offers a similar approach by providing a streamlined set of tools and language constructs that let you build robust software quickly, without getting tangled in unnecessary complexity.

2.4 Summary of Core Concepts

By now, you should have a clear picture of what Go is and why it is increasingly being adopted across industries. We've covered:

- **What Go is:** A modern, compiled programming language designed for simplicity, performance, and efficient concurrency.

- **History and Evolution:** Go was developed at Google to address real-world software challenges and has evolved steadily, gaining widespread industry adoption.

- **Reasons to Choose Go:** Its simplicity, performance, concurrency model, robust standard library, and strong ecosystem make it a compelling choice for modern software development.

In the following sections, we will transition from theory to practice—showing you how to set up your Go development environment and build your first Go applications. Let's move on to preparing your tools and getting your machine ready to run Go code.

3. Tools and Setup

Before you can dive into writing Go code, it's essential to set up a robust development environment. In this section, we will list the necessary tools, walk you through the installation process, and ensure your system is configured correctly for Go development.

3.1 Required Tools and Platforms

To follow along with this chapter and begin your journey into Go programming, you'll need the following:

- **Go Compiler and Toolchain:**
  The official Go distribution includes the compiler, package manager, and other essential tools. You can download it from the official Go website.

- **Text Editor or Integrated Development Environment (IDE):**
  While you can write Go code in any text editor, many developers prefer IDEs that offer syntax highlighting, code completion, and debugging tools. Popular choices include:

- o **Visual Studio Code (VS Code):** Highly customizable with Go extensions.

- o **GoLand:** A full-featured IDE from JetBrains, designed specifically for Go.

- o **Sublime Text/Atom:** Lightweight editors that can be configured for Go development.

- **Command Line Interface (CLI):**
A terminal or command prompt to run Go commands and manage your projects.

- **Version Control System:**
Git is the most commonly used system for version control, enabling you to track changes and collaborate with others. Installation instructions for Git can be found on the official Git website.

```
main.go

File   Edit   Selection   View   Go

EXAMPLE              main.go

EXAMPLE              package main
  go.mod               import fmt
  main.go
  server.go            func handler(w http.ResponseWriter,
  user.go                r *http.Request)
                         fmt.Frrintf(w, "Hello, World!")
                       }

                       func main()
                         http.HandleFunc("/, handler
                         http.ListenAndServe(nil)
                       }

                       fun
```

creenshot of a typical **Go** development setup with **VS Code**

3.2 Installing Go

Step 1: Downloading the Installer

1. **Visit the Official Website:**

    Navigate to golang.org/dl where you can find the latest
    stable version of Go for your operating system.

2. **Choose Your Platform:**

   Download the appropriate installer for Windows, macOS, or Linux. The installer includes all necessary tools, so you don't need to worry about manual configuration of the compiler.

3. **Run the Installer:**

   Follow the on-screen instructions to complete the installation. By default, Go is installed in a system directory, and environment variables are set automatically by the installer.

Step 2: Verifying the Installation

After installing, open your terminal or command prompt and run the following command to verify the installation:

```
bash
```

```
go version
```

You should see output indicating the version of Go installed (for example, go version go1.20 darwin/amd64).

3.3 Configuring Your Go Workspace

Go uses a workspace structure to manage your projects and dependencies. By default, your workspace will be located in a directory defined by the environment variable GOPATH. Here's how to set it up:

1. **Create a Workspace Directory:**
   Choose a location on your computer where you'll store your Go projects. For example, on macOS or Linux, you might create a directory called ~/go.

2. **Set the GOPATH Environment Variable:**
   On Unix-based systems, you can add the following lines to your shell configuration file (e.g., .bashrc or .zshrc):

```bash
export GOPATH=$HOME/go
export PATH=$PATH:$GOPATH/bin
```

On Windows, you can set environment variables through the System Properties > Advanced > Environment Variables interface.

3. **Verify Your Workspace:**

   Create a simple directory structure within your
   workspace:

bash

```
mkdir -p $GOPATH/src/hello
cd $GOPATH/src/hello
```

3.4 Setting Up Your Editor/IDE for Go

While you can use any text editor to write Go code,
configuring your environment with an IDE or editor that
supports Go can improve your productivity. Below are steps
for setting up Visual Studio Code (VS Code):

1. **Install VS Code:**

   Download and install VS Code from
   code.visualstudio.com.

2. **Install Go Extension:**

   Open VS Code, go to the Extensions view, and search
   for "Go". Install the extension provided by the Go
   team, which adds features such as code navigation, auto-
   completion, and debugging.

3. **Configure Go Tools:**

   The Go extension may prompt you to install additional tools (like gofmt, guru, and dlv for debugging). Accept these installations to ensure a seamless coding experience.

3.5 First "Hello, World!" Project Setup

Now that you have your Go environment configured, it's time to write your first Go program. Follow these steps:

1. **Create a New Directory:**

   Within your workspace, navigate to the project directory:

```bash
cd $GOPATH/src/hello
```

2. **Write the Code:**

   Create a file named main.go with the following content:

```go
package main

import "fmt"
```

```
// main is the entry point of the program
func main() {
    fmt.Println("Hello, World!")
}
```

3. Run the Program:

Open your terminal in the project directory and run:

```bash
```

```
go run main.go
```

You should see "Hello, World!" printed to the console.

4. Build the Program:

To build an executable file, run:

```bash
```

```
go build
```

This command creates an executable file (hello on Unix-based systems, hello.exe on Windows) that you can run independently.

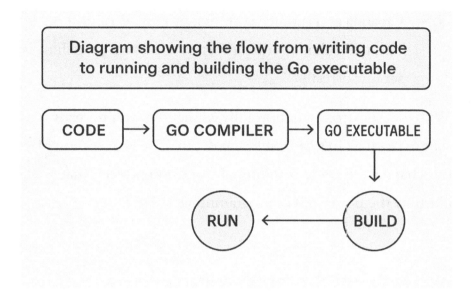

3.6 Recap of Tools and Setup

In summary, setting up your Go development environment involves:

- **Installing the Go toolchain:** Download and install from the official website.

- **Configuring your workspace:** Setting the GOPATH and organizing your project directories.

- **Choosing the right editor:** Using VS Code (or your preferred IDE) with Go extensions to boost productivity.

- **Creating and running your first project:** Writing a simple "Hello, World!" program to ensure everything is set up correctly.

With your environment now fully configured, you're ready to start exploring Go's capabilities in depth. The next section of this chapter will guide you through hands-on projects that illustrate the power of Go programming.

---

4. Hands-on Examples & Projects

In this extensive section, we will walk through practical examples and projects that reinforce the concepts discussed earlier. We start with the classic "Hello, World!" project and gradually build up to more advanced examples, illustrating how to write clean, efficient, and practical Go code. These projects are designed to build your confidence and introduce you to key programming paradigms in Go.

4.1 Project 1: Your First "Hello, World!" Program

Let's begin with our first project—writing the classic "Hello, World!" program. Although simple, this program establishes the basic structure of any Go application and reinforces the development process.

4.1.1 Writing the Code

Create a file named main.go in your project directory ($GOPATH/src/hello). Enter the following code:

```go
go
```

```go
package main

import "fmt"

// main is the entry point of the application.
func main() {
    // Print "Hello, World!" to the console.
    fmt.Println("Hello, World!")
}
```

4.1.2 Running the Program

Open your terminal in the project directory and execute:

```bash
bash
```

```bash
go run main.go
```

Expected Output:

Hello, World!

4.1.3 Explanation

- **Package Declaration:**

  The program begins with package main, which tells Go that this file is part of an executable package.

- **Import Statement:**

  The import "fmt" line includes the standard I/O package, which provides functions for formatting text.

- **Main Function:**

  The main function is where the execution of the program begins. Here, we call fmt.Println to output the string to the console.

This simple exercise lays the groundwork for understanding how Go programs are structured.

4.2 Project 2: Building a Basic Calculator

Next, we'll create a basic calculator to demonstrate Go's ability to handle user input, perform computations, and display results. This project will introduce you to variables, basic data types, and simple control structures.

4.2.1 Overview and Objectives

In this project, we will:

- Prompt the user to input two numbers.

- Perform basic arithmetic operations (addition, subtraction, multiplication, division).

- Display the results.

4.2.2 Code Implementation

Create a file named calculator.go and insert the following code:

```go

package main

import (
    "fmt"
    "log"
)

// main function to run the calculator
func main() {
```

```go
    var num1, num2 float64
    var operation string

    fmt.Println("Simple Calculator in Go")
    fmt.Print("Enter first number: ")
    if _, err := fmt.Scanln(&num1); err != nil {
        log.Fatal("Invalid input for first
number:", err)
    }

    fmt.Print("Enter second number: ")
    if _, err := fmt.Scanln(&num2); err != nil {
        log.Fatal("Invalid input for second
number:", err)
    }

    fmt.Print("Choose an operation (+, -, *, /): ")
    if _, err := fmt.Scanln(&operation); err !=
nil {
        log.Fatal("Invalid input for operation:",
err)
    }

    var result float64
    switch operation {
```

```
case "+":
    result = num1 + num2
case "-":
    result = num1 - num2
case "*":
    result = num1 * num2
case "/":
    if num2 == 0 {
        log.Fatal("Error: Division by zero is
not allowed.")
    }
    result = num1 / num2
default:
    log.Fatal("Unknown operation:",
operation)
}

    fmt.Printf("Result: %.2f\n", result)
}
```

4.2.3 Running the Calculator

Compile and run the calculator program with:

bash

go run calculator.go

Expected Behavior:

- The program prompts for two numbers.

- It then asks for an arithmetic operator.

- Finally, it displays the computed result.

4.2.4 Explanation

- **Input Handling:**
  We use fmt.Scanln to capture user input. Error
  handling is included to ensure the user provides valid
  input.

- **Switch Statement:**
  The switch statement cleanly handles different
  arithmetic operations.

- **Error Checking:**
  A division-by-zero check prevents runtime errors,
  illustrating how to write robust, defensive code.

4.3 Project 3: Developing a Simple To-Do List Application

In this project, we will create a simple command-line To-Do list application. This example will help you understand how to manage collections of data, use slices, and implement basic control flow logic.

4.3.1 Project Objectives

- Manage a list of tasks (adding, removing, listing).

- Use Go slices to dynamically handle an array of tasks.

- Practice writing functions to encapsulate functionality.

4.3.2 Code Implementation

Create a file called todo.go and insert the following code:

```go

package main

import (
    "bufio"
    "fmt"
    "os"
    "strings"
```

```go
)

// Global slice to store tasks
var tasks []string

// Function to display the list of tasks
func listTasks() {
    fmt.Println("\nYour To-Do List:")
    if len(tasks) == 0 {
        fmt.Println("  No tasks added yet.")
        return
    }
    for i, task := range tasks {
        fmt.Printf("  %d. %s\n", i+1, task)
    }
}

// Function to add a new task
func addTask(task string) {
    tasks = append(tasks, task)
    fmt.Println("Task added successfully!")
}

// Function to remove a task by its index
func removeTask(index int) {
    if index < 0 || index >= len(tasks) {
```

```go
        fmt.Println("Invalid task number.")
        return
    }
    tasks = append(tasks[:index],
tasks[index+1:]...)
    fmt.Println("Task removed successfully!")
}


func main() {
    reader := bufio.NewReader(os.Stdin)
    for {
        fmt.Println("\n--- To-Do List Menu ---")
        fmt.Println("1. List tasks")
        fmt.Println("2. Add a task")
        fmt.Println("3. Remove a task")
        fmt.Println("4. Exit")
        fmt.Print("Enter your choice (1-4): ")

        choiceInput, _ := reader.ReadString('\n')
        choiceInput =
strings.TrimSpace(choiceInput)

        switch choiceInput {
        case "1":
            listTasks()
        case "2":
```

```go
            fmt.Print("Enter the task
description: ")
            task, _ := reader.ReadString('\n')
            task = strings.TrimSpace(task)
            addTask(task)
        case "3":
            fmt.Print("Enter the task number to
remove: ")
            var num int
            if _, err := fmt.Scanf("%d\n", &num);
err != nil {
                fmt.Println("Invalid input.")
            } else {
                removeTask(num - 1)
            }
        case "4":
            fmt.Println("Exiting To-Do List.
Goodbye!")
            return
        default:
            fmt.Println("Invalid choice. Please
try again.")
        }
    }
}
```

4.3.3 Running the To-Do List Application

Run the application with:

bash

go run todo.go

Expected Behavior:

- The application displays a menu.

- Users can add, list, and remove tasks interactively.

- The application gracefully exits when chosen.

Diagram of the To-Do List application flow

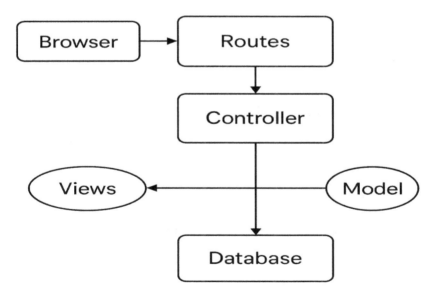

4.3.4 Explanation

- **Data Management:**

  Tasks are stored in a global slice, showcasing how to use slices to manage dynamic collections.

- **User Interaction:**

  The program employs bufio.NewReader for reading user input, providing a robust way to capture strings.

- **Modular Functions:**

  The functions listTasks(), addTask(), and removeTask() encapsulate functionality, illustrating the benefits of code modularity and reuse.

4.4 Project 4: Building a Simple HTTP Server

One of the most compelling features of Go is its built-in support for web development. In this project, we will build a basic HTTP server that responds to web requests with a "Hello, World!" message. This project demonstrates how Go can be used to create networked applications and web services.

4.4.1 Project Objectives

- Set up a basic HTTP server using Go's standard library.

- Handle HTTP requests and send responses.

- Explore how to serve dynamic content.

4.4.2 Code Implementation

Create a file called server.go with the following code:

```go

package main

import (
    "fmt"
    "log"
    "net/http"
)

// helloHandler handles HTTP requests and sends a
greeting.
func helloHandler(w http.ResponseWriter, r
*http.Request) {
    fmt.Fprintln(w, "Hello, World! Welcome to my
Go HTTP server.")
}
```

```
func main() {
    http.HandleFunc("/", helloHandler)
    fmt.Println("Starting server on port
8080...")
    if err := http.ListenAndServe(":8080", nil);
err != nil {
        log.Fatal("Server error:", err)
    }
}
```

4.4.3 Running the HTTP Server

1. **Run the Server:**

   Execute the command in your terminal:

```
bash
```

```
go run server.go
```

2. **Test the Server:**

   Open a web browser and navigate to
   http://localhost:8080. You should see the message
   "Hello, World! Welcome to my Go HTTP server."

4.4.4 Explanation

- **HTTP Package:**

  The code uses Go's standard net/http package, which
  provides HTTP client and server implementations.

- **Handler Functions:**

  helloHandler is registered to handle all requests to the root URL (/).

- **Server Execution:**

  The call to http.ListenAndServe starts the server on port 8080, listening for incoming connections and dispatching them to the registered handler.

4.5 Recap of Hands-on Projects

In this section, we built several projects that illustrate key aspects of Go programming:

- A simple "Hello, World!" program to establish basic structure.

- A calculator application that demonstrates user input, error handling, and control structures.

- A To-Do list application to work with slices, functions, and modular code.

- An HTTP server that introduces web development in Go.

Each project is designed not only to reinforce theoretical concepts but also to empower you to tackle real-world problems with Go.

---

5. Advanced Techniques & Optimization

After mastering the basics and building several practical projects, you may be eager to dive into advanced techniques. In this section, we explore strategies for optimizing your Go code, best practices for concurrency, and performance tuning tips that can help your applications scale efficiently.

5.1 Advanced Concurrency Patterns

Go's approach to concurrency is one of its most powerful features. Beyond basic goroutines and channels, advanced patterns such as worker pools, pipelines, and the use of the context package can help manage complex concurrent workflows.

5.1.1 Worker Pools

A worker pool is a design pattern that distributes tasks among a set of worker goroutines. This is particularly useful when you need to process a large number of tasks concurrently without overwhelming system resources.

Example: Worker Pool Implementation

```go

package main

import (
    "fmt"
    "sync"
    "time"
)

// worker processes tasks from the jobs channel
and sends results to the results channel.
func worker(id int, jobs <-chan int, results
chan<- int, wg *sync.WaitGroup) {
    defer wg.Done()
    for j := range jobs {
        fmt.Printf("Worker %d processing job
%d\n", id, j)
        time.Sleep(time.Millisecond * 500) //
simulate work
        results <- j * 2
    }
```

```go
}

func main() {
    const numJobs = 10
    jobs := make(chan int, numJobs)
    results := make(chan int, numJobs)
    var wg sync.WaitGroup

    // Start a pool of workers.
    for w := 1; w <= 3; w++ {
        wg.Add(1)
        go worker(w, jobs, results, &wg)
    }

    // Send jobs to the workers.
    for j := 1; j <= numJobs; j++ {
        jobs <- j
    }
    close(jobs)

    // Wait for all workers to finish.
    wg.Wait()
    close(results)

    // Display results.
    for result := range results {
```

```
        fmt.Println("Result:", result)
    }
}
```

5.1.2 Pipelines

Pipelines allow you to chain multiple processing stages, with each stage running in its own set of goroutines. This pattern is especially useful for data transformation tasks.

5.2 Performance Optimization Techniques

Optimizing Go applications often involves balancing resource usage and execution speed. Here are some best practices:

- **Profiling:**
  Use Go's built-in profiling tools (like pprof) to identify performance bottlenecks.

- **Efficient Data Structures:**
  Choose the right data structures for your tasks. For instance, use slices for dynamic arrays and maps for quick lookups.

- **Minimize Allocations:**
  Be mindful of memory allocations. Reuse objects where possible and avoid unnecessary ing.

- **Concurrency Tuning:**

  Adjust the number of goroutines based on workload
  and available CPU cores to avoid excessive context
  switching.

5.3 Code Snippets for Optimization

Below is an example demonstrating how to use pprof for
profiling a Go application:

```go

package main

import (
    "log"
    "net/http"
    _ "net/http/pprof" // Import for side-effect
of enabling pprof
)

func main() {
    // Start the pprof server in a separate
goroutine.
    go func() {
```

```
log.Println(http.ListenAndServe("localhost:6060",
nil))
    }()

    // Your application logic goes here.
    // ...
}
```

5.4 Trade-offs and Considerations

When applying advanced techniques, it's crucial to understand the trade-offs:

- **Complexity vs. Performance:**
  While advanced concurrency patterns can improve performance, they also add complexity. Always weigh the benefits against maintainability.

- **Resource Utilization:**
  Optimizing for speed might lead to higher memory usage, so consider the constraints of your deployment environment.

- **Scalability:**
  Design your applications to scale gracefully by adopting

patterns that allow you to increase concurrency without significant overhead.

---

6. Troubleshooting and Problem-Solving

Even the best developers encounter issues when learning a new language. In this section, we'll cover common challenges, how to debug Go code, and tips for solving problems that arise during development.

6.1 Common Challenges in Go Development

1. **Compilation Errors:**

   Often caused by syntax mistakes, missing packages, or type mismatches.

2. **Runtime Panics:**

   Issues such as nil pointer dereferences or out-of-bound slice access.

3. **Concurrency Bugs:**

   Race conditions and deadlocks are common pitfalls when working with goroutines and channels.

4. **Dependency Management:**

   Although Go modules simplify dependency management, version mismatches or missing modules can still occur.

6.2 Debugging Techniques

6.2.1 Using the Go Compiler

The Go compiler provides clear error messages that usually indicate the location and nature of the problem. Always read the error output carefully and refer to the Go documentation if necessary.

6.2.2 Debugging with Delve

Delve is a powerful debugger for Go that allows you to set breakpoints, inspect variables, and step through your code.

Basic Delve Usage Example:

1. **Install Delve:**

```bash

go install github.com/go-
delve/delve/cmd/dlv@latest
```

2. **Run Your Program with Delve:**

```
bash
```

```
dlv debug
```

3. **Use Commands:**

   Once in the Delve shell, you can use commands such as break main.main, continue, and print <variable>.

6.3 Troubleshooting Concurrency Issues

Concurrency can be challenging, but these tips can help:

- **Race Detector:**

  Run your code with the race detector enabled:

```
bash
```

```
go run -race main.go
```

This will help identify data races.

- **Logging:**

  Add logging statements in goroutines to track the flow of execution.

- **Simplify:**

  If concurrency bugs persist, try to reduce the code to a minimal example that reproduces the issue, then incrementally add complexity back.

6.4 Before-and-After: Fixing a Common Error

Scenario: A program panics due to accessing a nil slice element.

Before (Faulty Code):

```go

var data []int
fmt.Println(data[0])
```

After (Fixed Code):

```go

data := []int{1, 2, 3}
if len(data) > 0 {
    fmt.Println(data[0])
} else {
    fmt.Println("No data available.")
}
```

6.5 Summary of Troubleshooting Techniques

- **Error messages are your friends:** Read them carefully.

- Use debugging tools like Delve and the race detector.

- **Write defensive code:** Check for nil pointers, out-of-range indices, and proper error handling.

- **Consult the community:** Online forums, documentation, and peers can be invaluable resources.

---

7. Conclusion & Next Steps

As we wrap up this chapter on getting started with Go, it's time to reflect on the key takeaways and look ahead to further learning opportunities.

7.1 Recap of What You've Learned

In this chapter, we covered:

- **An Introduction to Go:**
  We defined Go, discussed its history and evolution, and explained why it has become a popular language for modern software development. You learned about its simplicity, performance, and built-in concurrency features that set it apart from other languages.

- **Setting Up Your Development Environment:**
  Detailed instructions for installing Go, configuring your workspace, and setting up your favorite IDE (with a focus on Visual Studio Code) were provided. You also

completed your first "Hello, World!" program to verify that your environment was correctly set up.

- **Hands-on Projects:**
  We walked through multiple projects—from a basic "Hello, World!" program and a calculator to a To-Do list application and an HTTP server. Each project was designed to illustrate key concepts in a practical, real-world context.

- **Advanced Techniques and Optimization:**
  For those looking to take their skills further, we explored advanced concurrency patterns, performance optimizations, and best practices for scalable Go programming.

- **Troubleshooting and Debugging:**
  Common pitfalls were discussed, and strategies for debugging, including using Delve and the race detector, were shared to help you overcome challenges as you develop your projects.

7.2 Next Steps in Your Go Journey

Now that you have a solid foundation in Go, consider these next steps to further your expertise:

- **Explore More Advanced Projects:**
  Build larger applications, perhaps a web service or a microservices architecture, to apply what you've learned in more complex scenarios.

- **Contribute to Open Source:**
  Join the vibrant Go community by contributing to open-source projects. This will help you gain experience, learn best practices, and connect with other developers.

- **Deepen Your Understanding:**
  Delve into topics like advanced concurrency patterns, network programming, and database integration. Online courses, books, and community forums can be invaluable.

- **Experiment and Innovate:**
  Try integrating Go with other technologies such as Docker, Kubernetes, or cloud services like AWS and

Google Cloud Platform. Experimentation will boost
your confidence and creativity.

7.3 Final Thoughts

Learning Go opens up a world of opportunities. Its efficiency,
simplicity, and robust toolchain make it a language that can
easily scale with your ambitions—from small hobby projects to
enterprise-level applications. Remember that the journey of
mastering a programming language is iterative: practice, learn
from your mistakes, and never hesitate to experiment with new
ideas.

Embrace the challenges and celebrate your progress. With the
foundation laid out in this chapter, you are well-equipped to
embark on more complex projects and further expand your
knowledge. Keep exploring, stay curious, and remember that
every programmer's journey starts with a single "Hello,
World!"

Chapter 2: Go Basics: Syntax, Variables, and Data Types

1. Introduction

In the world of programming, understanding the basics of a language is the foundation upon which you build your skills. For beginners and experienced developers alike, mastering the syntax, variables, and data types of any language is crucial. This chapter will introduce you to the core elements of the Go programming language, starting with its syntax and conventions, and progressing through key topics like variables, constants, and basic data types. We will explore how Go handles strings, numbers, and booleans in a straightforward way, helping you understand how to use them effectively in your programs.

Why Go?

Go, also known as Golang, is a statically typed, compiled language created by Google. It is renowned for its simplicity, performance, and scalability, making it an excellent choice for everything from web development to system programming. Go's syntax is designed to be clean and minimalistic, which allows developers to focus on writing efficient code without getting bogged down in complex syntax rules.

In this chapter, you will not only learn Go's basic syntax but also get hands-on experience with building a simple calculator application. This real-world project will help solidify the concepts we cover, ensuring that you can apply what you've learned to solve practical problems.

Key Concepts and Terminology

Before we dive in, let's briefly go over some key concepts and terms you'll encounter in this chapter:

- **Syntax:** The set of rules that define the structure of a program written in Go. It dictates how you write code that the Go compiler understands.

- **Variables:** A variable is a container for storing data values. Variables in Go must be declared with a specific type.

- **Constants:** Constants are similar to variables, but their values cannot be changed once set.

- **Data Types:** The classification of data that tells the compiler how the program should treat a specific piece of information (e.g., integer, string, boolean).

- **Basic Data Types:** Includes integers, floating-point numbers, booleans, and strings, each of which has a specific use in Go programming.

By the end of this chapter, you'll have a clear understanding of Go's syntax and how to work with basic data types, giving you a strong foundation for more advanced topics.

---

2. Core Concepts and Theory

2.1 Understanding Go Syntax and Conventions

Go's syntax is intentionally simple. It strives for clarity and minimalism while maintaining powerful capabilities. If you've worked with other programming languages, you will find that Go's syntax is easy to learn and intuitive to use.

2.1.1 Writing Your First Go Program

```go
package main

import "fmt"

func main() {
    fmt.Println("Hello, World!")
}
```

- **package main:** Every Go program starts with a package declaration. The main package is special because it defines the entry point of the program.

- **import "fmt":** The import statement allows you to bring in libraries that provide functionality. Here, we are importing the fmt (format) package, which is used for input/output operations like printing to the screen.

- **func main() { ... }:** The main function is where the execution of the program begins. It's like the heart of the Go application. Inside the main function, you can write the code you want to run.

- **fmt.Println:** This function prints the string "Hello, World!" to the console.

2.1.2 Basic Syntax Rules

1. **Semicolons:** In Go, semicolons are optional at the end of statements. The compiler automatically adds them when needed, making Go code less cluttered and easier to read.

2. **Braces {} for Block Statements:** Go uses curly braces {} to define code blocks, such as the body of functions or loops. There is no need for begin and end statements like in other languages.

3. **Variable and Function Declarations:** Go uses the var keyword for variable declarations, and func for function declarations. For example:

```go
var x int = 5
func add(a int, b int) int {
    return a + b
}
```

4. **Indentation:** Go requires consistent indentation for readability, but does not enforce any specific style, as long as it's consistent.

2.2 Variables, Constants, and Basic Data Types

Go is statically typed, which means every variable must have a type that is known at compile-time. However, Go is also quite flexible and offers shorthand ways to declare variables without explicitly stating the type.

2.2.1 Declaring Variables

In Go, you can declare variables in multiple ways, depending on the context.

1. **Explicit Type Declaration:**

```go
```

```go
var x int = 10
```

Here, we are declaring a variable x of type int and initializing it with a value of 10.

2. **Short Variable Declaration:**

Go allows you to use a shorthand declaration with the :=
operator, which automatically infers the type based on the
assigned value.

go

```go
x := 10 // Go knows that x is of type int
```

3. **Multiple Variables:**

You can declare multiple variables at once:

go

```go
var x, y int = 1, 2
```

Or with shorthand:

go

```go
x, y := 1, 2
```

2.2.2 Constants

In Go, constants are declared with the const keyword and, like
variables, must have a type. Constants are similar to variables,
but their values cannot be changed once set.

go

```go
const pi = 3.14
```

You can also specify a type for constants, though Go can often infer it:

```go

const gravity float64 = 9.8
```

2.2.3 Data Types in Go

Go provides several built-in types, but here we'll focus on the basic data types you'll use most often.

- **Integers:** These are used for whole numbers. Go supports several integer types, including:

    o int (the default, platform-dependent size)

    o int8, int16, int32, int64 (for specific sizes)

    o uint, uint8, uint16, uint32, uint64 (unsigned integers)

- **Floating-Point Numbers:** Used for numbers with decimal points. Go provides two types:

    o float32, float64 (the latter is the default for floating-point numbers).

- **Booleans:** A simple type used to represent true or false.

- **Strings:** Strings in Go are sequences of characters enclosed in double quotes. You can use strings for everything from messages to file paths.

go

```go
var name string = "Go"
var age int = 10
var temperature float64 = 36.6
var isActive bool = true
```

2.3 Working with Strings, Numbers, and Booleans

Now that we understand how to declare variables and constants, let's explore how to work with the most common types in Go: strings, numbers, and booleans.

2.3.1 Strings in Go

Go strings are immutable, meaning once they are created, their values cannot be changed. However, you can manipulate strings in various ways.

Here's how you can declare and manipulate strings:

go

```go
package main

import "fmt"

func main() {
    var greeting string = "Hello"
    var name string = "World"
    message := greeting + ", " + name + "!" //
Concatenate strings
    fmt.Println(message)
}
```

In this example:

- The + operator is used to concatenate strings.

- fmt.Println prints the concatenated result to the console.

You can also use Go's fmt.Sprintf for more complex formatting:

```go
go
```

```go
fmt.Sprintf("Hello, %s!", name) // Format string
```

2.3.2 Working with Numbers

Go allows you to perform arithmetic operations on integers and floating-point numbers. Let's look at basic operations:

```go
go

package main

import "fmt"

func main() {
    var x int = 10
    var y int = 3

    fmt.Println("Sum:", x + y)
    fmt.Println("Difference:", x - y)
    fmt.Println("Product:", x * y)
    fmt.Println("Quotient:", x / y)
    fmt.Println("Remainder:", x % y)

    var f1 float64 = 3.14
    var f2 float64 = 1.59
    fmt.Println("Float Sum:", f1 + f2)
}
```

Here, we:

- Perform basic arithmetic operations (addition, subtraction, multiplication, division, modulus).

- Work with float64 types for decimal values.

2.3.3 Booleans

Booleans are a crucial part of decision-making in programs. They represent truth values and can only be true or false.

```go
package main

import "fmt"

func main() {
    var isEven bool = true
    var isPrime bool = false

    fmt.Println("Is Even?", isEven)
    fmt.Println("Is Prime?", isPrime)
}
```

Booleans are often used in if conditions to make decisions in the code, as we'll see in our calculator project.

---

3. Tools and Setup

To follow along with the examples in this chapter, you'll need to set up your Go development environment. In this section, we will guide you through the tools and platforms required, and provide step-by-step instructions for installing and configuring Go.

3.1 Required Tools

1. **Go Programming Language:** You need the Go language installed on your machine. You can download it from the official Go website.

2. **Text Editor or IDE:** While you can write Go code in any text editor, using an IDE can help with code completion, syntax highlighting, and debugging. Recommended IDEs include:

    o **Visual Studio Code** (VS Code) with the Go extension

    o **GoLand** (from JetBrains)

3. **Command Line Interface (CLI):** You will need a terminal or command prompt to run Go commands and test your code.

3.2 Setting Up Go on Your Machine

Follow these steps to install Go on your system:

Step 1: Install Go

- Go to Go's Downloads Page and select the version appropriate for your operating system (Windows, macOS, or Linux).

- Follow the installation instructions for your platform.

Step 2: Verify Installation

Once installed, open a terminal or command prompt and type:

```bash
```

```
go version
```

You should see the Go version displayed, confirming that the installation was successful.

Step 3: Set Up Go Workspace

Go uses a workspace to manage your code and dependencies. By default, the Go workspace is located in your home directory under ~/go (or C:\Go on Windows). You can set a custom workspace by modifying the GOPATH environment variable.

3.3 Setting Up Visual Studio Code

1. **Install VS Code:** Download and install <u>Visual Studio Code</u>.

2. **Install Go Extension:** Launch VS Code, go to the Extensions view (left sidebar), search for the "Go" extension, and install it.

3. **Configure Go Tools:** The Go extension may prompt you to install tools like gofmt, gopls, and others. Allow the installation to streamline your development.

---

4. Hands-on Examples & Projects

Now that we have covered Go's syntax, variables, constants, and basic data types, it's time to get hands-on! In this section, we will build a **simple calculator** that demonstrates how to work with variables, constants, strings, numbers, and booleans.

4.1 Building a Simple Calculator

Let's create a simple calculator that can perform basic arithmetic operations such as addition, subtraction, multiplication, and division. We'll allow the user to input two numbers and choose an operation to perform.

Step 1: Define the Program Structure

We will:

1. Prompt the user for input.

2. Perform calculations based on the user's choice of operation.

3. Display the result.

Step 2: Code Implementation

```go
go

package main

import "fmt"

func main() {
    var num1, num2 float64
    var operation string

    fmt.Println("Simple Calculator")

    // Get user input for the first number
```

```go
fmt.Print("Enter first number: ")
fmt.Scanln(&num1)

// Get user input for the second number
fmt.Print("Enter second number: ")
fmt.Scanln(&num2)

// Get user input for the operation
fmt.Print("Enter operation (+, -, *, /): ")
fmt.Scanln(&operation)

var result float64

// Perform calculation based on the chosen operation
switch operation {
case "+":
    result = num1 + num2
case "-":
    result = num1 - num2
case "*":
    result = num1 * num2
case "/":
    if num2 != 0 {
        result = num1 / num2
    } else {
```

```
            fmt.Println("Error: Cannot divide by
zero.")
                return
        }
    default:
        fmt.Println("Invalid operation.")
        return
    }

    // Display the result
    fmt.Printf("Result: %.2f\n", result)
}
```

Step 3: Explanation

- **Variables:** We declare num1 and num2 as float64 to store the user's input numbers, and operation as a string to store the operation.

- **Switch Statement:** Based on the user's choice of operation, we use a switch statement to perform the appropriate calculation.

- **Error Handling:** We check if the user attempts to divide by zero and display an error message if so.

Step 4: Running the Calculator

To run the program, open your terminal, navigate to the project folder, and execute:

bash

```
go run calculator.go
```

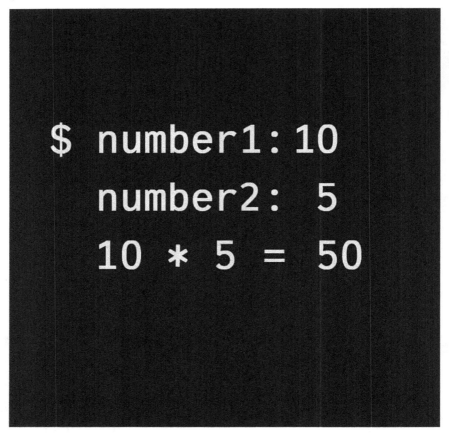

```
$ number1: 10
number2:  5
10 * 5 = 50
```

4.2 Refining the Calculator

This basic calculator can be improved by adding more functionality. For example, we can add support for more complex operations like exponentiation, or even implement a loop to allow the user to perform multiple calculations without restarting the program.

---

5. Advanced Techniques & Optimization

Now that you've learned how to work with Go's basic syntax, variables, and data types, let's explore some advanced techniques and optimization strategies that can help you write more efficient, maintainable code.

5.1 Optimizing Performance

Go is known for its speed and efficiency, but there are always ways to optimize your programs. Here are a few strategies:

- **Use of Go's Built-In Garbage Collection:**
  Go's garbage collector handles memory management automatically, but understanding its behavior and managing resources carefully can improve performance.

- **Minimize Memory Allocations:**

  Reuse variables and data structures instead of allocating new ones unnecessarily.

- **Avoid Premature Optimization:**

  Start with clear, simple code. Use Go's built-in profiling tools like pprof to identify bottlenecks later on.

---

6. Troubleshooting and Problem-Solving

As you develop your programs, you may encounter various issues. Let's look at some common problems and how to solve them.

6.1 Common Errors

1. **Type Mismatches:**

   Go is a statically typed language, so trying to assign a value of one type to a variable of another type will result in a compilation error.

```go

var num int = "string"  // Error: mismatched
types
```

2. **Division by Zero:**

Division by zero is a common error in many programs. Always check for zero before performing division, as we did in our calculator project.

---

7. Conclusion & Next Steps

In this chapter, you have learned about Go's syntax, how to declare variables and constants, and how to work with basic data types like strings, numbers, and booleans. We also built a simple calculator to apply these concepts.

Next Steps:

- **Explore More Projects:**
  Challenge yourself by building more complex projects like a unit converter or a basic text-based game.

- **Deepen Your Understanding of Go's Features:**
  Go offers many more advanced features like interfaces, concurrency with goroutines, and web development with its built-in packages. Continue exploring!

With this strong foundation, you're now ready to tackle more advanced Go topics and expand your skills to build more sophisticated applications. Happy coding!

Chapter 3: Control Structures and Error Handling in Go

1. Introduction

In any programming language, control structures form the backbone of the decision-making and flow of logic in a program. They help you define how your program reacts to different conditions, how it repeats actions, and how it handles errors. Understanding control structures is crucial for building efficient, flexible, and functional software. In this chapter, we'll dive into the essential control structures in Go, namely conditionals, loops, and error handling, along with practical examples to demonstrate how they work in real-world applications.

Why Do Control Structures Matter?

Control structures enable you to create programs that respond to different conditions or situations in a dynamic way. Whether you're building an application that processes user input, a server that handles multiple client requests, or a tool that interacts with files, you will frequently encounter conditions and data that need to be evaluated to determine the next step in your program.

Similarly, error handling ensures that your program can gracefully handle unexpected issues without crashing. Error handling is essential for ensuring that your software is robust and reliable.

This chapter covers three main areas:

- **Conditionals:** How to make decisions in your program using if, else, and switch statements.

- **Loops:** How to iterate over data and perform repetitive tasks using the for loop.

- **Error Handling:** How Go's approach to error handling makes your programs safer and more predictable.

After going through this chapter, you'll be able to use these constructs in Go to build programs that respond intelligently to different situations and handle unexpected conditions effectively.

Key Concepts and Terminology

Before we begin, let's define a few essential terms:

- **Conditionals:** Constructs that let you perform actions based on conditions, such as if, else, and switch.

- **Loops:** Constructs that allow you to repeat a block of code multiple times. In Go, the for loop is the primary loop structure.

- **Error Handling:** The process of anticipating, detecting, and managing errors in a program to prevent crashes and unexpected behaviors. Go uses a simple but powerful model for error handling.

We will now explore these concepts in greater detail.

---

2. Core Concepts and Theory

2.1 Conditionals: if, else, and switch Statements

Conditionals allow you to control the flow of your program by checking conditions (such as whether a number is positive, whether a file exists, or whether a user has the right permissions). Go provides three main ways to implement conditionals: if, else, and switch.

2.1.1 if Statements

The if statement is the most basic form of conditional, allowing you to execute code only if a condition is true.

Basic Syntax of if

```go

if condition {
    // code to execute if condition is true
}
```

Here's an example where we check if a number is positive:

```go

package main

import "fmt"

func main() {
    number := 10

    if number > 0 {
        fmt.Println("The number is positive.")
    }
}
```

In this example, because the number is greater than zero, the program prints "The number is positive.".

if-else Statements

You can extend if statements with an else block, which allows you to define actions if the condition is false.

```go

if condition {
    // code if true
} else {
    // code if false
}
```

Example:

```go

package main

import "fmt"

func main() {
    number := -5

    if number > 0 {
```

```go
        fmt.Println("The number is positive.")
    } else {
        fmt.Println("The number is negative or
zero.")
    }
}
```

In this case, since number is negative, the program will print "The number is negative or zero.".

2.1.2 switch Statements

The switch statement provides a cleaner way to handle multiple conditions. It's essentially a more readable version of a series of if-else statements when you need to check several possible cases.

Basic Syntax of switch

```go
go


switch expression {
case value1:
    // code if expression == value1
case value2:
    // code if expression == value2
default:
    // code if no case matches
```

```
}
```

Example:

```go
go

package main

import "fmt"

func main() {
    day := 3

    switch day {
    case 1:
        fmt.Println("Monday")
    case 2:
        fmt.Println("Tuesday")
    case 3:
        fmt.Println("Wednesday")
    default:
        fmt.Println("Invalid day")
    }
}
```

This program will output "Wednesday" since day is equal to 3.

2.1.3 switch with fallthrough

In Go, switch does not automatically fall through to the next case (unlike in C or other languages). However, you can use the fallthrough keyword to force the execution to continue to the next case.

Example:

```go
package main

import "fmt"

func main() {
    day := 2

    switch day {
    case 1:
        fmt.Println("Monday")
    case 2:
        fmt.Println("Tuesday")
        fallthrough
    case 3:
        fmt.Println("Wednesday")
    default:
        fmt.Println("Invalid day")
    }
```

```
}
```

Here, the program will print:

```
mathematica
```

```
Tuesday
Wednesday
```

This is because fallthrough forces execution into the next case after printing "Tuesday".

2.2 Looping with for: Iterating Over Data

Loops allow you to repeat a block of code multiple times. In Go, there is only one loop construct: the for loop. While it is versatile, you can use it in different ways to simulate other looping constructs.

2.2.1 Basic for Loop

The basic for loop consists of three parts: initialization, condition, and post.

```go
go
```

```
for initialization; condition; post {
    // code to repeat
```

```go
}
```

Example:

```go
package main

import "fmt"

func main() {
    for i := 0; i < 5; i++ {
        fmt.Println(i)
    }
}
```

This code prints numbers from 0 to 4, because the condition i < 5 is checked before each iteration.

2.2.2 Infinite Loops

You can create an infinite loop by omitting the condition part of the for statement.

```go
for {
    // infinite loop code
}
```

This will run indefinitely until a break statement or external condition forces it to exit.

Example:

```go
package main

import "fmt"

func main() {
    i := 0
    for {
        fmt.Println(i)
        i++
        if i > 3 {
            break
        }
    }
}
```

This will print:

0

1

2

3

2.2.3 for Loop with range

The range keyword allows you to iterate over collections like arrays, slices, and maps in Go. It simplifies the process of looping through each element in these collections.

Example with a slice:

```go
package main

import "fmt"

func main() {
    numbers := []int{1, 2, 3, 4, 5}

    for index, value := range numbers {
        fmt.Printf("Index: %d, Value: %d\n", index, value)
    }
}
```

This will output:

yaml

```
Index: 0, Value: 1
Index: 1, Value: 2
Index: 2, Value: 3
Index: 3, Value: 4
Index: 4, Value: 5
```

You can also omit the index or value if you don't need them.

2.3 Understanding Error Handling in Go

Error handling is one of the defining features of Go. Instead of using exceptions like many other programming languages, Go uses a simple model where functions return an error value along with the result. If the error is nil, the function worked as expected; otherwise, the caller can handle the error appropriately.

2.3.1 Basic Error Handling

In Go, functions that might fail return an error type as the last return value. Here's an example:

go

```
package main
```

```go
import (
    "fmt"
    "errors"
)

func divide(a, b int) (int, error) {
    if b == 0 {
        return 0, errors.New("cannot divide by
zero")
    }
    return a / b, nil
}

func main() {
    result, err := divide(10, 0)
    if err != nil {
        fmt.Println("Error:", err)
    } else {
        fmt.Println("Result:", result)
    }
}
```

In this example:

- The divide function returns an error if the denominator is zero.

- We check if the error is nil. If not, we print the error message.

2.3.2 Custom Errors

You can define your own custom error types by implementing the Error() method for a struct.

```go

package main

import (
    "fmt"
)

type DivisionError struct {
    Message string
}

func (e *DivisionError) Error() string {
    return e.Message
}

func divide(a, b int) (int, error) {
    if b == 0 {
```

```go
        return 0, &DivisionError{Message: "cannot
divide by zero"}
    }
    return a / b, nil
}

func main() {
    result, err := divide(10, 0)
    if err != nil {
        fmt.Println("Error:", err)
    } else {
        fmt.Println("Result:", result)
    }
}
```

Here, we defined a custom error DivisionError that includes a message. If the error occurs, we return an instance of that error.

---

3. Tools and Setup

To follow along with the examples in this chapter, you will need a Go environment set up on your machine. Below are the steps for setting up Go, writing, and running the examples.

3.1 Required Tools

- **Go Programming Language:** You need to have Go installed on your computer. You can download it from Go's official website.

- **Text Editor or IDE:** A text editor such as **Visual Studio Code** or an IDE like **GoLand** will be useful for writing Go code.

- **Command Line Interface:** You will need to use the terminal or command prompt to run your Go programs.

3.2 Installing Go

1. Download the latest Go version for your operating system from Go's official website.

2. Follow the installation instructions for your platform (Windows, macOS, or Linux).

3. Verify your installation by running the following command in your terminal:

```bash

go version
```

You should see the installed Go version if everything is set up correctly.

3.3 Setting Up the Go Environment

Go uses a workspace structure to manage your Go programs. By default, your workspace is stored in the ~/go directory on Unix-based systems, or C:\Go on Windows.

- To customize your workspace, you can modify the GOPATH environment variable.

Step-by-Step Setup:

1. **Create a Go Workspace Directory:**
   Create a new directory for your Go projects, for example, ~/go.

2. **Set the GOPATH Environment Variable:**
   On Linux/macOS, add the following lines to your shell profile (e.g., .bashrc or .zshrc):

```bash
export GOPATH=$HOME/go
export PATH=$PATH:$GOPATH/bin
```

On Windows, set the GOPATH through System Properties > Environment Variables.

---

4. Hands-on Examples & Projects

4.1 Creating a Command-Line Tool with Error Feedback

Let's now create a more practical tool, a command-line tool that checks if a given number is prime, with error handling in place for invalid inputs.

Step 1: Defining the Tool

We will:

1. Accept a number as input.

2. Check if the number is prime.

3. Provide error feedback if the input is not a valid number.

Step 2: Code Implementation

go

```go
package main

import (
    "fmt"
    "strconv"
    "os"
)

func isPrime(n int) bool {
    if n <= 1 {
        return false
    }
    for i := 2; i*i <= n; i++ {
        if n%i == 0 {
            return false
        }
    }
    return true
}

func main() {
    if len(os.Args) < 2 {
        fmt.Println("Error: Please provide a number.")
        return
    }
```

```go
    input := os.Args[1]
    number, err := strconv.Atoi(input)
    if err != nil {
        fmt.Println("Error: Invalid number
format.")
        return
    }

    if isPrime(number) {
        fmt.Printf("%d is a prime number.\n",
number)
    } else {
        fmt.Printf("%d is not a prime number.\n",
number)
    }
}
```

Step 3: Explanation

- **os.Args** is used to capture command-line arguments.

- **strconv.Atoi** converts the string input to an integer, handling any invalid input gracefully.

- **isPrime function** checks if the number is prime.

Step 4: Running the Tool

To run the tool:

1. Save the code as primecheck.go.

2. Open the terminal and navigate to the directory containing the file.

3. Run the following command:

```bash

go run primecheck.go 29
```

This will output:

```csharp

29 is a prime number.
```

If an invalid input is provided:

```bash

go run primecheck.go abc
```

The output will be:

```typescript

Error: Invalid number format.
```

5. Advanced Techniques & Optimization

5.1 Optimizing Performance

While Go provides powerful tools for handling control structures and errors, performance can always be optimized. Below are some strategies to improve the efficiency of your code.

- **Minimize Memory Allocations:** Avoid unnecessary memory allocations by reusing variables and using pointers when possible.

- **Efficient Error Handling:** Handle errors as early as possible, and avoid excessive error checking in tight loops.

5.2 Best Practices

- **Keep Functions Small:** Functions should do one thing and do it well. This makes your code easier to read and maintain.

- **Use Early Returns:** Handle errors and edge cases early in the function to avoid deep nesting of logic.

6. Troubleshooting and Problem-Solving

6.1 Common Challenges

- **Mismatched Data Types:** Always check that your variables are of the correct type before performing operations.

- **Infinite Loops:** Ensure that the loop termination condition is correct to prevent infinite loops.

6.2 Debugging Tips

- Use the built-in fmt.Println for basic debugging.

- Use Go's **pprof** tool for performance profiling.

---

7. Conclusion & Next Steps

In this chapter, we covered the essential control structures in Go, including conditionals (if, else, and switch), loops (for), and error handling. We also demonstrated these concepts through practical examples, like the command-line prime checker.

Next Steps

- **Expand the Prime Checker:** Add more features to the prime checker, such as checking for factors or handling larger inputs more efficiently.

- **Dive Deeper into Go's Error Handling:** Explore custom error types and how to design error-handling strategies for larger applications.

With these tools and techniques under your belt, you're now ready to tackle more complex programming tasks in Go!

Chapter 4: Functions and Modular Code in Go

1. Introduction

In the world of software development, modularity is a key principle that allows code to be organized, reusable, and maintainable. One of the fundamental ways to achieve modularity is through the use of functions. Functions allow us to break down complex tasks into smaller, more manageable pieces, making it easier to test, debug, and understand code. In this chapter, we will delve into Go's approach to defining and calling functions, understanding function parameters and return types, and managing the scope and lifetime of variables. We'll also explore how to structure your Go code to be modular, making it easier to build scalable applications.

Why Functions Matter

Functions are at the heart of programming in Go, just as they are in almost every other language. They allow us to:

- **Encapsulate logic:** Instead of writing the same logic multiple times, you can define it in one place and call it whenever needed.

- **Promote reusability:** Functions can be reused across different parts of a program, reducing duplication and improving code maintainability.

- **Improve readability and structure:** A well-structured program with functions is much easier to read and maintain. Functions allow you to break down complex processes into logical steps.

In Go, functions are not just a way to organize your code but also a powerful feature for building efficient and scalable software. This chapter will provide you with a thorough understanding of how functions work in Go, and how to leverage them to write better code.

Key Concepts and Terminology

Before we dive into the details of functions in Go, let's define some key terms and concepts that we'll be using throughout the chapter:

- **Function Definition:** The process of creating a function with a specific name, parameters, return types, and body.

- **Function Call:** The process of invoking or executing a function within a program.

- **Parameters:** The input values that a function accepts to perform its task.

- **Return Types:** The type of value(s) a function returns after execution.

- **Scope:** The visibility and lifetime of variables in a program, which is determined by where they are declared (e.g., inside a function, in the global scope).

- **Modular Code:** A design approach that divides code into separate, reusable functions or modules that can be combined to achieve a desired outcome.

With these concepts in mind, we are ready to explore the specifics of Go functions and how to make your code modular and maintainable.

2. Core Concepts and Theory

2.1 Defining and Calling Functions in Go

In Go, defining and calling functions is straightforward. A function consists of the following parts:

1. **The function signature**: This includes the function name, parameters, and return type.

2. **The function body**: This contains the code that is executed when the function is called.

2.1.1 Function Syntax

Here's the basic syntax for defining a function in Go:

```go

func functionName(parameter1 type, parameter2 type) returnType {
    // function body
}
```

For example, here's how to define a simple function that adds two integers:

```go

package main
```

```go
import "fmt"

// Function definition
func add(a int, b int) int {
    return a + b
}

func main() {
    result := add(3, 4)
    fmt.Println("Sum:", result) // Output: Sum: 7
}
```

In this example:

- **func add(a int, b int) int** is the function signature.

    o add is the name of the function.

    o a and b are parameters of type int.

    o The function returns a value of type int.

- **return a + b** is the body of the function that performs the addition.

2.1.2 Function Calls

Once a function is defined, you can call it by simply using its name and providing the necessary arguments. For example, in the main function, we call add(3, 4) to compute the sum of 3 and 4.

2.2 Understanding Function Parameters and Return Types

Go functions can accept multiple parameters and return multiple values. Let's break this down further.

2.2.1 Function Parameters

In Go, you define parameters within the parentheses after the function name. Each parameter must be followed by its type.

go

```go
func multiply(a int, b int) int {
    return a * b
}
```

You can also define parameters with the same type in a more concise way:

go

```go
func multiply(a, b int) int {
    return a * b
```

}

2.2.2 Function Return Types

Functions in Go can return one or more values. To specify multiple return types, separate them by commas in the function signature.

```go
go
```

```go
func divide(a, b int) (int, int) {
    quotient := a / b
    remainder := a % b
    return quotient, remainder
}
```

In the example above, the divide function returns both the quotient and the remainder of two integers. When calling this function, you can receive both return values:

```go
go
```

```go
quotient, remainder := divide(10, 3)
fmt.Println("Quotient:", quotient, "Remainder:", remainder)
```

This would output:

```
makefile
```

```
Quotient: 3 Remainder: 1
```

2.2.3 Named Return Values

Go also allows you to name the return values, which can make your code clearer and allow for simplified return statements.

```go
func divide(a, b int) (quotient, remainder int) {
    quotient = a / b
    remainder = a % b
    return
}
```

Now, you don't need to explicitly write return quotient, remainder at the end of the function. Go will automatically return the named values.

2.3 Scope and Lifetime of Variables

Variables in Go can have different scopes depending on where they are declared. Understanding the scope and lifetime of variables is critical to writing modular and error-free code.

2.3.1 Local vs Global Scope

- **Local Variables:** These are variables declared inside a function and can only be accessed within that function.

- **Global Variables:** These are variables declared outside any function (typically at the top of the file) and can be accessed throughout the entire file.

Example of a local variable:

```go
func greet() {
    message := "Hello, Go!" // Local variable
    fmt.Println(message)
}

func main() {
    greet()
    // fmt.Println(message) // Error: message is
not defined in this scope
}
```

Here, message is a local variable in the greet function and is not accessible outside of it.

Example of a global variable:

```go
```

```go
package main

import "fmt"

var globalMessage = "Hello, Global!"

func greet() {
    fmt.Println(globalMessage) // Accessible in
this function
}

func main() {
    greet()
    fmt.Println(globalMessage) // Accessible in
main as well
}
```

2.3.2 Variable Lifetime

The **lifetime** of a variable refers to how long the variable exists in memory. A local variable only exists during the execution of the function it was declared in, and it is destroyed once the function completes. Global variables, on the other hand, persist for the lifetime of the program.

2.4 Modular Code in Go

Modular code refers to the practice of dividing code into smaller, reusable units, such as functions or packages. This makes the code easier to maintain, test, and scale. In Go, functions are the primary way to achieve modularity.

2.4.1 Benefits of Modular Code

- **Maintainability:** Changes to a function only affect the code inside that function, making maintenance easier.

- **Reusability:** Once a function is defined, it can be used in many places, reducing the need for duplicate code.

- **Testability:** Each function can be tested independently, ensuring that each part of the program works as expected.

---

3. Tools and Setup

To follow along with the examples in this chapter, you will need a Go development environment set up on your system. Here's how to get started:

3.1 Required Tools

- **Go Programming Language:** Download and install the latest version of Go from Go's official website.

- **Text Editor or IDE:** You can use any text editor or Integrated Development Environment (IDE) to write Go code, but we recommend using one with Go support, such as:

  - **Visual Studio Code (VS Code)**

  - **GoLand**

  - **Sublime Text**

- **Command Line Interface (CLI):** You will need a terminal (macOS/Linux) or Command Prompt (Windows) to run your Go programs.

3.2 Setting Up Go

1. **Install Go:**

   Follow the installation instructions for your platform on the Go Downloads Page.

2. **Verify Installation:**

   After installation, verify that Go is installed correctly by running the following command in your terminal:

```
bash
```

```
go version
```

You should see the version of Go that is installed on your machine.

3. **Set Up Workspace (Optional):**

   By default, Go creates a workspace in the $HOME/go directory on macOS/Linux or C:\Go on Windows. You can change the workspace location by setting the GOPATH environment variable.

3.3 Setting Up Visual Studio Code

1. **Install Visual Studio Code (VS Code):**

   Download and install VS Code from here.

2. **Install the Go Extension:**

   Open VS Code, go to the Extensions view (click on the Extensions icon in the left sidebar), and search for the Go extension. Install it to enable Go syntax highlighting, code completion, and debugging support.

3. **Install Go Tools:**

   After installing the Go extension, VS Code will prompt you to install the necessary Go tools, such as gopls, gofmt, and others. Allow these installations to ensure a smooth development experience.

---

4. Hands-on Examples & Projects

Now that you have the tools set up, let's dive into the practical side of Go programming. In this section, we'll create a modular code base for a small application that calculates and manages simple geometric shapes such as rectangles and circles.

4.1 Building a Modular Geometry Calculator

In this project, we will:

1. Define functions to calculate the area and perimeter of various shapes.

2. Structure the code into modules to keep it organized and reusable.

Step 1: Define the Geometry Module

Let's start by creating a module for handling rectangles. We will define functions to calculate the area and perimeter of a rectangle.

```go
package geometry

// Rectangle struct to represent a rectangle
type Rectangle struct {
    Width, Height float64
}

// Area function to calculate the area of the
rectangle
func (r Rectangle) Area() float64 {
    return r.Width * r.Height
}

// Perimeter function to calculate the perimeter
of the rectangle
func (r Rectangle) Perimeter() float64 {
    return 2 * (r.Width + r.Height)
}
```

Step 2: Define the Circle Module

Next, let's create a module for circles, where we calculate the area and circumference.

```go
package geometry

import "math"

// Circle struct to represent a circle
type Circle struct {
    Radius float64
}

// Area function to calculate the area of the
circle
func (c Circle) Area() float64 {
    return math.Pi * c.Radius * c.Radius
}

// Circumference function to calculate the
circumference of the circle
func (c Circle) Circumference() float64 {
    return 2 * math.Pi * c.Radius
}
```
Step 3: Main Program to Use the Geometry Module

Now, we'll create a main.go file to tie everything together and use the geometry module.

```go
package main

import (
    "fmt"
    "your_project/geometry"
)

func main() {
    // Create a rectangle instance
    rect := geometry.Rectangle{Width: 5, Height: 10}

    fmt.Printf("Rectangle Area: %.2f\n", rect.Area())
    fmt.Printf("Rectangle Perimeter: %.2f\n", rect.Perimeter())

    // Create a circle instance
    circle := geometry.Circle{Radius: 7}

    fmt.Printf("Circle Area: %.2f\n", circle.Area())
```

```
    fmt.Printf("Circle Circumference: %.2f\n",
circle.Circumference())
}
```

Step 4: Running the Program

To run this program:

1. Save the geometry code in a geometry folder.

2. Save the main.go file in the root folder of your project.

3. Open your terminal and navigate to your project directory.

4. Run the following command:

```bash

go run main.go
```

This will output:

```mathematica

Rectangle Area: 50.00
Rectangle Perimeter: 30.00
Circle Area: 153.94
Circle Circumference: 43.98
```

4.2 Refactoring the Code

As the program grows, you might find that you need to add more shapes or features. Here's a quick overview of how you can refactor the code to keep it modular and easy to maintain:

- **Separation of Concerns:** Each shape (Rectangle, Circle) should have its own methods for calculating properties like area and perimeter.

- **Reusable Code:** Once functions like Area and Perimeter are defined, they can be reused across multiple shapes.

- **Scalability:** You can add more shapes (e.g., triangles, squares) by creating new structs and functions without affecting existing code.

---

5. Advanced Techniques & Optimization

5.1 Advanced Function Usage

5.1.1 Function Overloading

While Go doesn't support traditional function overloading (i.e., defining multiple functions with the same name but different parameters), you can achieve similar behavior using interface types or variadic functions.

5.1.2 High-Order Functions

Go allows you to pass functions as arguments to other functions or return them from functions, enabling functional programming patterns.

```go
package main

import "fmt"

func applyOperation(a, b int, op func(int, int) int) int {
    return op(a, b)
}

func add(a, b int) int {
    return a + b
}

func main() {
    result := applyOperation(3, 4, add)
```

```
    fmt.Println("Result:", result) // Output:
Result: 7
}
```

5.2 Optimizing Function Performance

1. **Avoid Redundant Calculations:** Cache values that are reused within a function to minimize unnecessary computations.

2. **Minimize Memory Usage:** Pass large objects (like arrays or slices) by reference rather than by value to avoid excessive ing.

---

6. Troubleshooting and Problem-Solving

6.1 Common Issues

- **Nil Pointer Dereference:** Ensure that you don't call methods on nil pointers, especially when working with structs.

- **Misused Return Values:** Always check that the correct number of return values is captured when calling functions that return multiple results.

6.2 Debugging Tips

- **Use fmt.Println for Debugging:** Print out variable values to trace the flow of your program and catch unexpected results.

- **Use the Go Debugger (delve):** For more complex debugging, the delve tool allows you to set breakpoints, step through code, and inspect variables.

---

7. Conclusion & Next Steps

In this chapter, we've explored the fundamental concepts of defining and calling functions in Go, as well as understanding parameters, return types, and scope. We also built a modular code base for a small geometric calculator, demonstrating how to structure your code to make it scalable and maintainable.

Next Steps:

- **Expand the Geometry Calculator:** Add more shapes, such as triangles or polygons, to your calculator.

- **Dive Deeper into High-Order Functions:** Experiment with passing functions as arguments to build more flexible and reusable code.

- **Explore Go's Standard Library:** Investigate Go's rich standard library to see how modularity is applied in practice.

With a solid understanding of functions and modularity, you're well on your way to writing more complex, maintainable Go programs. Happy coding!

Chapter 5: Data Structures: Arrays, Slices, and Maps in Go

1. Introduction

In software development, choosing the right data structure is essential for writing efficient and maintainable code. Data structures are the building blocks for organizing and storing data, making it easy to access, manipulate, and process. Go, like many programming languages, provides several fundamental data structures to help you handle and organize data effectively. In this chapter, we will explore three of the most commonly used data structures in Go: arrays, slices, and maps. Each of these structures offers different benefits, and understanding their characteristics is critical for writing optimal Go code.

Why Data Structures Matter

When you're working on a software project, data is a core part of your application. Whether you're processing a list of user inputs, storing configurations, or building a web service that handles requests and responses, how you organize this data affects your program's performance and scalability. Choosing the right data structure can:

- Optimize your program's speed, ensuring that operations like searching, sorting, and updating data are performed efficiently.

- Make your code more readable and maintainable by organizing it logically.

- Help you avoid pitfalls such as memory inefficiency, poor performance, and complex code logic.

Key Concepts and Terminology

Before we dive deeper into each data structure, let's define a few important terms:

- **Array:** A fixed-size collection of elements of the same type. In Go, the size of an array is determined when it is created and cannot be changed later.

- **Slice:** A dynamic, flexible view over an array. Slices in Go allow you to manage collections of data more efficiently than arrays, as they can grow and shrink in size.

- **Map:** A collection of key-value pairs, where each key is unique, and each key is mapped to a value. Maps provide fast lookups based on the key, making them suitable for efficient data retrieval.

In this chapter, you'll learn how to:

- Work with arrays and slices, including their creation, manipulation, and potential pitfalls.

- Use maps to store and retrieve data efficiently.

- Apply best practices for managing memory and optimizing performance when working with these data structures.

- Build a hands-on project—a simple inventory management system—to put your knowledge of these data structures into practice.

By the end of this chapter, you'll have a solid understanding of how to use arrays, slices, and maps in Go, and be able to build modular and efficient programs.

2. Core Concepts and Theory

2.1 Working with Arrays in Go

Arrays are a basic data structure in Go that stores a fixed-size sequence of elements of the same type. Arrays are valuable for simple, static collections, but they have some limitations when it comes to flexibility and memory management.

2.1.1 Declaring and Initializing Arrays

In Go, you declare arrays using the var keyword, followed by the array name, type, and size:

```go

```

```go
var arr [5]int
```

This declares an array named arr with 5 elements, all of type int. The size of an array is part of its type, which means arrays of different sizes are considered distinct types in Go.

You can also initialize arrays with values:

```go

```

```go
arr := [5]int{1, 2, 3, 4, 5}
```

This initializes an array with the values 1, 2, 3, 4, and 5.

2.1.2 Accessing and Modifying Array Elements

You can access and modify elements in an array using an index:

```go
```

```go
arr[0] = 10 // Modify the first element of the
array
fmt.Println(arr[0]) // Output: 10
```

Arrays in Go are zero-indexed, so the first element is at index 0, the second at index 1, and so on.

2.1.3 Array Length

You can determine the length of an array using the len function:

```go
```

```go
fmt.Println(len(arr)) // Output: 5
```

The length of the array is fixed and cannot be changed after initialization.

2.1.4 Pitfalls of Arrays

- **Fixed Size:** One of the main limitations of arrays is that their size is fixed once they are created. If you need to change the size of a collection dynamically, arrays may not be the best option.

- **Memory Overhead:** Arrays in Go are copied by value when passed to functions, which can result in unnecessary memory overhead for large arrays.

2.2 Working with Slices in Go

Slices are a more flexible and powerful alternative to arrays. Unlike arrays, slices do not have a fixed size. They are built on top of arrays and provide a dynamically resizable view into an underlying array.

2.2.1 Declaring and Initializing Slices

You can declare a slice using the [] notation, which does not require specifying the size:

go

```
var slice []int
```
You can also initialize a slice with values:

go

```go
slice := []int{1, 2, 3, 4, 5}
```

2.2.2 Slicing an Array or Another Slice

Slices can be created from arrays or other slices using a range of indices:

```go

```

```go
arr := [5]int{1, 2, 3, 4, 5}
slice := arr[1:4] // Slice from index 1 to 3 (not
including index 4)
fmt.Println(slice) // Output: [2 3 4]
```

2.2.3 Modifying Slices

Slicing an array or another slice creates a new slice that references the underlying array. Modifications to the slice will affect the original array:

```go

```

```go
slice[0] = 10
fmt.Println(arr) // Output: [1 10 3 4 5]
```

2.2.4 Slice Capacity and Length

Slices have two important properties:

- **Length (len):** The number of elements the slice contains.

- **Capacity (cap):** The number of elements the slice can hold before needing to allocate a new array.

You can access these properties using the len and cap functions:

```go
```

```go
fmt.Println(len(slice)) // Length of the slice
fmt.Println(cap(slice)) // Capacity of the slice
```

2.2.5 Resizing Slices

You can use the append function to add elements to a slice, which will automatically resize the underlying array if necessary:

```go
```

```go
slice = append(slice, 6)
fmt.Println(slice) // Output: [2 3 4 6]
```

The append function is crucial for dynamically adjusting the size of slices without needing to manually manage the underlying array.

2.2.6 Pitfalls of Slices

- **Capacity Management:** When using slices with large datasets, it's essential to be mindful of their capacity to avoid unnecessary allocations.

- **Aliasing:** Slices share the same underlying array, so modifying one slice can affect other slices that share the same array. This can lead to unexpected bugs if not managed properly.

2.3 Working with Maps in Go

Maps are another essential data structure in Go that allow you to store and retrieve data using key-value pairs. Maps are highly efficient for looking up values based on a key.

2.3.1 Declaring and Initializing Maps

You can declare a map using the make function or by using the map literal syntax:

```go

// Declaring a map using the make function
m := make(map[string]int)
```

```go
// Declaring and initializing a map using a
literal
m := map[string]int{
    "apple":  5,
    "banana": 3,
    "cherry": 7,
}
```

2.3.2 Accessing and Modifying Map Elements

You can access and modify map values using the key:

go

```go
m["apple"] = 10 // Modify the value associated
with the "apple" key
fmt.Println(m["apple"]) // Output: 10
```

2.3.3 Checking for Key Existence

When accessing a map, Go allows you to check if a key exists using the second return value:

go

```go
value, exists := m["banana"]
if exists {
    fmt.Println("Value:", value)
} else {
    fmt.Println("Key not found")
```

```go
}
```

2.3.4 Deleting Map Elements

You can remove elements from a map using the delete function:

```go
delete(m, "cherry") // Removes the key "cherry"
from the map
```

2.3.5 Pitfalls of Maps

- **Uninitialized Maps:** Maps must be initialized before use. If you try to access a nil map, Go will panic.

- **Key Collision:** If two different values are assigned to the same key, the most recent value will overwrite the previous one.

- **No Ordering:** Maps do not guarantee any order for their keys. If you need ordered data, you may need to sort the keys manually.

2.4 Best Practices for Memory and Performance

When working with arrays, slices, and maps, memory and performance considerations are essential. Here are some best practices for efficient data structure use in Go:

2.4.1 Arrays and Slices

- **Use Slices for Flexibility:** If you need to work with a collection that can grow or shrink in size, always prefer slices over arrays.

- **Avoid Excessive Memory Allocation:** Slices can reallocate memory when their capacity is exceeded. Use the cap() function to monitor the capacity and avoid unnecessary reallocations.

- **Reuse Memory:** When slicing arrays, remember that slices share memory with the original array. Use this feature to minimize memory allocations.

2.4.2 Maps

- **Use Maps for Fast Lookups:** Maps provide average constant-time complexity for lookups, making them ideal for scenarios where quick access to data is required.

- **Preallocate Map Capacity:** If you know the expected size of the map, you can preallocate capacity to avoid resizing during execution:

```go
m := make(map[string]int, 100) // Preallocate
space for 100 elements
```

---

3. Tools and Setup

To follow along with the examples in this chapter, you will need a Go development environment set up. Here's how to get started:

3.1 Required Tools

1. **Go Programming Language:**
   Download and install the latest version of Go from Go's official website.

2. **Text Editor or IDE:**
   You can use any text editor or Integrated Development

Environment (IDE) to write Go code, but we recommend using one with Go support, such as:

- o **Visual Studio Code (VS Code)**

- o **GoLand**

- o **Sublime Text**

3. **Command Line Interface (CLI):**
A terminal (macOS/Linux) or Command Prompt (Windows) is required to run your Go programs.

3.2 Setting Up Go

1. **Install Go:**
Follow the installation instructions for your platform on the Go Downloads Page.

2. **Verify Installation:**
After installation, verify that Go is correctly installed by running:

```bash
```

```
go version
```

3. **Setting Up Your Workspace:**
Go uses a workspace structure, typically located in ~/go

on macOS/Linux or C:\Go on Windows. You can customize the workspace by setting the GOPATH environment variable.

3.3 Setting Up Visual Studio Code

1. **Install Visual Studio Code (VS Code):**

   Download and install VS Code from here.

2. **Install the Go Extension:**

   Open VS Code, go to the Extensions view (click the Extensions icon), and search for the Go extension. Install it for Go syntax highlighting, code completion, and debugging.

---

4. Hands-on Examples & Projects

4.1 Developing a Simple Inventory Management System

Now that we've covered arrays, slices, and maps, let's put these concepts to use by building a simple inventory management system. This system will allow us to add, remove, and display inventory items using a combination of arrays, slices, and maps.

Step 1: Define Inventory Structure

```go
package main

import "fmt"

// Define a map to store inventory items with
product names as keys
var inventory = make(map[string]int)

func addItem(name string, quantity int) {
    inventory[name] += quantity
}

func removeItem(name string, quantity int) {
    if currentQuantity, exists :=
inventory[name]; exists {
        if currentQuantity >= quantity {
            inventory[name] -= quantity
        } else {
            fmt.Println("Error: Not enough stock
to remove")
```

```go
        }
    } else {
        fmt.Println("Error: Item not found in
inventory")
    }
}

func displayInventory() {
    fmt.Println("Inventory:")
    for name, quantity := range inventory {
        fmt.Printf("%s: %d\n", name, quantity)
    }
}
```

Step 2: Main Function to Interact with Inventory

```go
go

func main() {
    addItem("Apple", 10)
    addItem("Banana", 5)
    addItem("Orange", 3)

    displayInventory()

    removeItem("Banana", 3)
    displayInventory()
```

```
    removeItem("Grapes", 2) // Error: Item not
found in inventory
}
```

Step 3: Running the Program

1. Save the code in a file named inventory.go.

2. Open your terminal and navigate to the directory containing the file.

3. Run the following command:

```
bash

go run inventory.go
This will output:
makefile

Inventory:
Apple: 10
Banana: 5
Orange: 3
Inventory:
Apple: 10
Banana: 2
Orange: 3
Error: Item not found in inventory
```

5. Advanced Techniques & Optimization

5.1 Advanced Array and Slice Usage

1. **Multi-Dimensional Arrays:**

   Go allows you to create multi-dimensional arrays, which are useful for representing matrices or grids. For example:

```go
var matrix [3][3]int
```

2. **Slice Resizing:**

   Use the append function to resize slices dynamically.

5.2 Best Practices for Maps

1. **Preallocate Capacity:**

   When creating large maps, preallocate memory for the expected size using make(map[string]int, 100) to reduce reallocation overhead.

2. **Use Pointer Types for Map Values:**

   If map values are large structures, consider using pointers to avoid ing the entire object when the map is accessed.

6. Troubleshooting and Problem-Solving

6.1 Common Challenges

1. **Nil Map Access:**

   Always initialize a map before accessing it. Trying to access a nil map will cause a runtime panic.

2. **Slice Capacity:**

   Be mindful of slice capacity and avoid excessive reallocations. You can use the cap() function to monitor this.

6.2 Debugging Tips

- **Print Statements:**

  Use fmt.Println() to print the state of arrays, slices, and maps at different points in your program to understand their current values.

7. Conclusion & Next Steps

In this chapter, we covered the fundamental data structures in Go: arrays, slices, and maps. We explored their creation, manipulation, and common pitfalls, as well as best practices for memory and performance. Through the hands-on example of an inventory management system, you applied these concepts in a practical scenario.

Next Steps:

- **Experiment with More Complex Data Structures:**
  Try implementing your own data structures, like linked lists or stacks, using arrays, slices, and maps.

- **Explore Go's Concurrency Features:**
  Learn how to use goroutines and channels to work with these data structures concurrently.

By mastering arrays, slices, and maps, you are now equipped to manage and manipulate data efficiently in Go. Happy coding!

Chapter 6: Structs, Interfaces, and Go's Type System

1. Introduction

In Go, one of the most powerful aspects of the language is its type system, which helps you model real-world scenarios in an efficient and readable way. The type system in Go is built around two key features: **structs** and **interfaces**. These allow you to define custom data structures and behavior, making Go both flexible and highly performant.

Understanding how to design and use structs and interfaces is essential for any Go developer, whether you're building a web service, a CLI application, or system software. In this chapter, we will explore these key features of Go's type system, along with best practices, pitfalls to avoid, and how you can use them to create modular, maintainable, and efficient code.

Why Structs and Interfaces Matter

When you're building any complex software, you need the ability to represent data and actions in a structured way. This is where **structs** come in: they allow you to group related data together into a single unit, making it easier to manage.

However, just grouping data isn't enough. You also need a way to define behavior and interact with different data types in a polymorphic way (i.e., allow different data types to be treated as one type while maintaining their own unique functionality). This is where **interfaces** come into play. With interfaces, you can define a contract that other types can implement, enabling polymorphism and greater flexibility in your code.

In this chapter, we'll walk through:

- Creating and using **structs** to represent data.

- Understanding **interfaces** and how they enable polymorphism in Go.

- Exploring **embedding and composition**, two powerful techniques that extend the flexibility of structs and interfaces.

- Building a **hands-on project** to design a basic system for handling user data.

By the end of the chapter, you'll have a deep understanding of Go's type system and how to apply it effectively in your programs.

Key Concepts and Terminology

Before diving into the details, let's quickly define some essential terms:

- **Struct:** A user-defined type that groups together variables (called fields) into a single entity. Each field in a struct can have a different type.

- **Interface:** A type that specifies a set of methods. A type is considered to implement an interface if it provides definitions for all the methods in the interface.

- **Embedding:** A technique in Go where one struct includes another struct as a field, allowing the embedded struct's methods to be accessed directly from the outer struct.

- **Polymorphism:** A concept that allows different types to be treated as the same type based on shared behavior (methods in Go).

With these concepts in mind, let's explore how to define and work with structs and interfaces in Go.

---

2. Core Concepts and Theory

2.1 Creating and Using Structs

Structs are the building blocks for custom data types in Go. They allow you to group related data together, making it easy to manage and manipulate complex data structures.

2.1.1 Declaring a Struct

In Go, you define a struct using the type keyword followed by the struct name and the struct fields:

go

```go
type Person struct {
    Name    string
    Age     int
    Address string
}
```

Here, the Person struct has three fields: Name, Age, and Address, each with their own type (string, int, string).

2.1.2 Initializing and Using Structs

Once a struct is defined, you can create instances of that struct in various ways:

1. Using Named Fields:

```go

p := Person{Name: "John", Age: 30, Address: "123 Main St"}
```

2. Using Positional Fields:

```go

p := Person{"John", 30, "123 Main St"}
```
This syntax works if the fields are in the same order as defined in the struct. However, it's generally better to use named fields to avoid mistakes.

3. Default Values:

If a struct is declared without initialization, all fields are set to their zero values (e.g., "" for strings, 0 for integers).

```go

```

```go
var p Person // All fields are initialized to
zero values
```

2.1.3 Accessing Struct Fields

You can access the fields of a struct using the dot (.) operator:

```go
```

```go
fmt.Println(p.Name)    // Output: John
fmt.Println(p.Age)     // Output: 30
fmt.Println(p.Address) // Output: 123 Main St
```

2.1.4 Methods with Structs

In Go, you can define methods on structs. Methods allow you to define behavior that operates on the struct's data.

```go
```

```go
func (p *Person) Greet() {
    fmt.Printf("Hello, my name is %s and I am %d
years old.\n", p.Name, p.Age)
}
```

Here, Greet is a method defined on the Person struct. The method has a receiver (p *Person) which allows the method to operate on an instance of Person.

You can call methods on structs like this:

```go
go
```

```go
p.Greet() // Output: Hello, my name is John and I
am 30 years old.
```

2.2 Introduction to Interfaces and Polymorphism in Go

An interface is a type that defines a set of method signatures. A type implements an interface by providing concrete implementations of those methods. Unlike other languages, Go does not require explicit declarations of intent to implement an interface. A type implements an interface implicitly simply by having the required methods.

2.2.1 Declaring an Interface

In Go, you declare an interface using the type keyword:

```go
go
```

```go
type Greeter interface {
    Greet() string
}
```

This Greeter interface defines a single method Greet, which returns a string.

2.2.2 Implementing an Interface

If a struct has a method that matches the method signature in the interface, it is considered to implement that interface automatically. There is no need to explicitly declare that a struct implements an interface.

For example, let's define a struct and implement the Greeter interface:

```go
type Person struct {
    Name string
}

func (p Person) Greet() string {
    return "Hello, my name is " + p.Name
}
```

Here, Person automatically implements the Greeter interface because it has a method Greet that matches the method signature in the interface.

2.2.3 Using Interfaces

You can now use the Greeter interface as a type in your code. Since Person implements Greeter, you can assign an instance of Person to a Greeter variable.

go

```go
var g Greeter
g = Person{Name: "John"}
fmt.Println(g.Greet()) // Output: Hello, my name is John
```

2.2.4 Polymorphism with Interfaces

Interfaces enable polymorphism in Go. This allows you to treat different types as the same type if they implement the same interface.

go

```go
type Animal interface {
    Speak() string
}

type Dog struct{}
type Cat struct{}

func (d Dog) Speak() string {
    return "Woof"
```

```
}

func (c Cat) Speak() string {
    return "Meow"
}

func main() {
    var animal Animal

    animal = Dog{}
    fmt.Println(animal.Speak()) // Output: Woof

    animal = Cat{}
    fmt.Println(animal.Speak()) // Output: Meow
}
```

Here, both Dog and Cat implement the Animal interface, so they can be assigned to a variable of type Animal, and we can invoke the Speak method polymorphically.

2.3 Embedding and Composition

Go supports a form of composition called **embedding**, where one struct can include another as a field. This allows a struct to "inherit" methods from another struct without using traditional inheritance.

2.3.1 Struct Embedding

With embedding, you can access methods of the embedded struct directly from the outer struct. This allows for a composition of functionality.

```go

type Address struct {
    Street string
    City   string
}

type Person struct {
    Name    string
    Address // Embedded struct
}

func main() {
    p := Person{
        Name: "John",
        Address: Address{
            Street: "123 Main St",
            City:   "GoCity",
```

```
        },
    }


    fmt.Println(p.Name)      // Output: John
    fmt.Println(p.Street)    // Output: 123 Main
St (accessing the embedded struct's field)
    fmt.Println(p.City)      // Output: GoCity
}
```

In this example, Person embeds Address, which means Person can directly access the fields and methods of Address.

2.3.2 Composition over Inheritance

Go emphasizes **composition** rather than traditional inheritance. Instead of inheriting behavior, you compose new structs by embedding existing ones. This avoids many of the complexities and pitfalls associated with inheritance, such as tight coupling and difficulties in extending functionality.

---

3. Tools and Setup

3.1 Required Tools

To follow along with the examples in this chapter, you need the following tools installed on your machine:

- **Go Programming Language:** Go must be installed on your machine. You can download it from Go's official website.

- **Text Editor or IDE:** You can use any text editor to write Go code, but it is highly recommended to use an editor with Go support, such as:

  o **Visual Studio Code** with the Go extension

  o **GoLand**

  o **Sublime Text** with Go support

- **Command Line Interface (CLI):** You will need a terminal or command prompt to run your Go code.

3.2 Setting Up Go

1. **Download and Install Go:**
   Visit Go's Downloads Page and follow the instructions for your operating system.

2. **Verify Installation:**
   After installing Go, open a terminal and type the following command to verify that Go is installed correctly:

```bash
```

```
go version
```

This command should display the installed Go version.

3. **Setting Up Your Workspace:**

    Go uses a workspace structure for organizing code. By default, Go creates a workspace in the ~/go directory (or C:\Go on Windows). You can set your own workspace path by modifying the GOPATH environment variable.

3.3 Setting Up Visual Studio Code (VS Code)

1. **Install VS Code:**

    Download and install Visual Studio Code.

2. **Install the Go Extension:**

    Open VS Code, go to the Extensions view, search for the Go extension, and install it. This will enable syntax highlighting, code completion, and debugging for Go.

4. Hands-on Examples & Projects

4.1 Designing a Basic System for Handling User Data

In this section, we will design a basic system to handle user data using structs and interfaces. Our system will allow us to create user profiles and display user information.

Step 1: Defining the User Struct

```go
package main

import "fmt"

type User struct {
    Name      string
    Age       int
    Email     string
    IsActive  bool
}
```

Here, the User struct contains basic fields for name, age, email, and a boolean indicating whether the user is active.

Step 2: Defining the Display Method

We'll add a method to the User struct that prints the user's information:

```go
func (u User) Display() {
    fmt.Println("Name:", u.Name)
    fmt.Println("Age:", u.Age)
    fmt.Println("Email:", u.Email)
    fmt.Println("Active Status:", u.IsActive)
}
```

Step 3: Creating a User Manager Interface

Now, let's define an interface for managing users. The interface will have a method Display that every user must implement.

```go
type UserManager interface {
    Display()
}
```

Step 4: Implementing the Interface

Since User already has a Display method, it automatically implements the UserManager interface.

Step 5: Managing Users

Let's create a function to manage users and display their
information:

```go
func manageUser(u UserManager) {
    u.Display()
}

func main() {
    user := User{
        Name:      "Alice",
        Age:       30,
        Email:     "alice@example.com",
        IsActive:  true,
    }

    manageUser(user) // Call manageUser with user
as an argument
}
```

Step 6: Running the Program

To run the program, save the code to a file named main.go,
open your terminal, and use the following command:

```bash
go run main.go
```

The program will output:

```yaml
Name: Alice
Age: 30
Email: alice@example.com
Active Status: true
```

---

5. Advanced Techniques & Optimization

5.1 Advanced Struct Usage

5.1.1 Struct Methods with Pointers

You can define methods that modify the state of a struct by using a pointer receiver. This allows the method to modify the struct directly:

```go
func (u *User) Activate() {
    u.IsActive = true
}
```

5.1.2 Nested Structs

Go allows nesting structs, which is useful when you need to represent more complex data structures.

```go
type Address struct {
    Street, City, State string
}

type User struct {
    Name    string
    Address Address
}
```

---

6. Troubleshooting and Problem-Solving

6.1 Common Challenges

- **Nil Pointer Dereference:** Always check if a pointer is nil before dereferencing it.

- **Interface Implementation Errors:** If your type doesn't implement an interface, Go will not throw an explicit error, but will silently fail to compile the program.

6.2 Debugging Tips

- **Print Statements:** Use fmt.Println() to debug the contents of structs and interfaces at various stages of your program.

- **Go Debugger (Delve):** Use the Delve debugger to set breakpoints and step through your code.

---

7. Conclusion & Next Steps

In this chapter, we've covered the fundamental concepts of structs, interfaces, and Go's type system. You've learned how to:

- Create and use structs to represent data.

- Use interfaces to enable polymorphism and abstract behavior.

- Understand embedding and composition for better code reuse and organization.

- Apply these concepts in a real-world example by designing a basic user data management system.

Next Steps:

- **Experiment with More Complex Systems:** Extend the user data system by adding more functionality, like updating user profiles or handling multiple users.

- **Explore Go's Concurrency Features:** Learn how to implement structs and interfaces in concurrent programming using goroutines and channels.

By mastering structs, interfaces, and Go's type system, you'll be well on your way to writing modular, maintainable, and efficient Go programs. Happy coding!

Chapter 7: Concurrency: Goroutines and Channels in Go

1. Introduction

Concurrency is one of the most powerful features of modern programming languages, allowing programs to execute multiple tasks simultaneously, thereby improving performance and responsiveness. In Go, concurrency is made simple and efficient through its powerful constructs, **goroutines** and **channels**. These tools are central to Go's design philosophy, making it easy to build highly concurrent systems that scale well with modern hardware.

Why is Concurrency Important?

Concurrency allows multiple tasks to run in parallel or in a non-blocking way, making it an essential technique for improving the efficiency of software. Many modern applications, from web servers to data processing systems, require the ability to handle multiple operations at once. Without concurrency, these tasks would have to be processed one after another, resulting in slower performance.

For instance, a web server handling many client requests might have to process each request sequentially without concurrency, resulting in a bottleneck. By leveraging concurrency, the server can handle multiple requests at once, ensuring quicker response times.

In Go, concurrency is a first-class citizen, and its simplicity and efficiency make it one of the most popular choices for concurrent programming.

Key Concepts and Terminology

Before diving into the specifics, let's define some key concepts related to concurrency:

- **Concurrency**: The ability of a program to handle multiple tasks simultaneously. This can be achieved either through parallel execution on multiple CPU cores or by switching between tasks in a single thread of execution.

- **Goroutines**: A lightweight thread of execution in Go. Goroutines are managed by the Go runtime, and they provide a simple and efficient way to perform concurrent tasks. They are much lighter than threads in traditional operating systems, enabling the creation of thousands or even millions of goroutines in a program.

- **Channels**: A way to communicate between goroutines. Channels provide a mechanism for safely passing data between concurrently running tasks. They ensure that data is synchronized between goroutines without the need for locks or other synchronization mechanisms.

- **Synchronization**: The process of coordinating the execution of multiple goroutines to ensure that data is accessed and modified safely.

In this chapter, we will explore:

- **Goroutines**: How to create and manage goroutines for concurrent execution.

- **Channels**: How to use channels to communicate and synchronize goroutines.

- **Best Practices and Pitfalls:** Tips for writing efficient and reliable concurrent Go programs.

- **Hands-on Project:** We will build a simple concurrent web scraper, applying goroutines and channels to handle multiple tasks concurrently.

Let's dive deeper into these concepts and explore how they can be applied to write efficient concurrent programs in Go.

---

2. Core Concepts and Theory

2.1 What is Concurrency and Why is It Important?

Concurrency, in simple terms, is the concept of performing multiple tasks at the same time. While many people confuse concurrency with parallelism, the key difference is that concurrency is about managing multiple tasks that can potentially run at the same time, while parallelism involves running those tasks simultaneously on multiple processors or cores.

In Go, concurrency is supported through **goroutines** and **channels**. Goroutines enable your program to perform multiple tasks simultaneously, and channels provide a safe way to communicate between these tasks.

2.1.1 Why Concurrency is Useful in Go

- **Parallelism**: Go makes it simple to take advantage of multi-core processors by running goroutines concurrently. Go's runtime scheduler assigns goroutines to different CPU cores, achieving parallelism.

- **Efficient I/O Operations**: Go's concurrency model is particularly beneficial for I/O-bound tasks like web scraping, network requests, or file handling. You can perform many I/O operations concurrently without blocking the main thread.

- **Responsive Programs**: In interactive applications or web servers, concurrency allows you to keep the program responsive by performing background tasks (such as handling multiple user requests) while the main application continues to run.

2.2 Introduction to Goroutines

A **goroutine** is a lightweight thread of execution in Go. You can think of it as a way to execute functions concurrently without dealing with the complexity of threads. Goroutines are managed by the Go runtime and are much lighter than traditional threads, making them easy to create and manage.

2.2.1 Creating a Goroutine

Creating a goroutine is simple. You use the go keyword before a function call, and Go will run that function in a new goroutine concurrently:

```
go
```

```
go myFunction()
```
This starts myFunction as a goroutine, allowing the program to continue executing other code while myFunction runs in the background.

2.2.2 Example of Goroutines

Let's look at a basic example of using goroutines to perform two tasks concurrently.

```
go
```

```go
package main

import (
    "fmt"
    "time"
)

func task1() {
    time.Sleep(2 * time.Second)
    fmt.Println("Task 1 completed")
}

func task2() {
    time.Sleep(1 * time.Second)
    fmt.Println("Task 2 completed")
}

func main() {
    go task1() // Start task1 as a goroutine
    go task2() // Start task2 as a goroutine

    // Wait for goroutines to complete
    time.Sleep(3 * time.Second)
}
```

In this example:

- task1 and task2 run concurrently.

- We use time.Sleep to ensure the main function waits long enough for the goroutines to complete before the program terminates.

2.2.3 Managing Goroutines

While go creates a goroutine, you often need to synchronize or wait for these goroutines to finish before the program exits. One simple way to manage goroutines is by using the sync.WaitGroup from the sync package.

```go
package main

import (
    "fmt"
    "sync"
)

func task(wg *sync.WaitGroup) {
    defer wg.Done()
    fmt.Println("Task completed")
}
```

```
func main() {
    var wg sync.WaitGroup
    wg.Add(1)

    go task(&wg)

    wg.Wait() // Wait for all goroutines to
finish
    fmt.Println("Main program finished")
}
```

Here, sync.WaitGroup is used to wait for the goroutine to finish before exiting the main program. This is a common pattern for managing goroutines in Go.

2.3 Communication Using Channels

Goroutines can communicate with each other using **channels**. A channel allows you to send and receive data between goroutines in a safe and synchronized manner.

2.3.1 Declaring and Using Channels

You declare a channel using the chan keyword. Channels are typed, meaning you specify what type of data the channel will carry (e.g., chan int for an integer channel).

```go
```

```go
ch := make(chan int) // Create an integer channel
```

You can send data into a channel using the <- operator:

```go
```

```go
ch <- 42 // Send value 42 into the channel
```

And you can receive data from the channel like this:

```go
```

```go
value := <-ch // Receive value from the channel
```

2.3.2 Example of Channel Usage

Let's see an example where we use channels to pass data between goroutines:

```go
```

```go
package main

import (
    "fmt"
)

func calculateSum(a, b int, ch chan int) {
    sum := a + b
```

```
    ch <- sum // Send the result into the channel
}

func main() {
    ch := make(chan int)

    go calculateSum(5, 3, ch) // Start goroutine
to calculate sum

    result := <-ch // Receive the result from the
channel
    fmt.Println("Sum:", result)
}
```

In this example:

- We start a goroutine that calculates the sum of two numbers.

- The result is sent to the channel ch, and the main function waits to receive it.

2.3.3 Buffered Channels

By default, channels are unbuffered, meaning a send operation on a channel will block until there is a receiver. You can create a **buffered channel** that allows sending and receiving data without blocking until the buffer is full:

```go
go
```

```go
ch := make(chan int, 2) // Create a buffered
channel with a capacity of 2
```

You can send two values into this channel without blocking:

```go
go
```

```go
ch <- 1
ch <- 2
```

However, if you try to send a third value without receiving from the channel first, the program will block.

2.4 Best Practices and Pitfalls in Concurrent Programming

While Go makes concurrency easy to implement, there are some best practices and potential pitfalls to watch out for.

2.4.1 Best Practices

- **Limit Goroutine Creation:** While goroutines are lightweight, creating too many goroutines can still overwhelm the system. Use worker pools or manage the number of active goroutines to avoid resource exhaustion.

- **Avoid Shared Memory Access:** When goroutines share data, use channels for communication instead of shared memory, to avoid race conditions and complex synchronization.

- **Use sync.WaitGroup or sync.Mutex:** These tools help you manage goroutines and synchronize shared resources. sync.WaitGroup is useful for waiting for multiple goroutines to finish, while sync.Mutex is used to protect shared resources.

2.4.2 Common Pitfalls

- **Deadlocks:** A deadlock occurs when two or more goroutines are waiting for each other to release resources, causing the program to freeze. Be mindful of how goroutines interact with each other and ensure proper synchronization.

- **Race Conditions:** A race condition happens when multiple goroutines access shared data concurrently, leading to unpredictable results. Always use channels or synchronization mechanisms to safely access shared resources.

---

3. Tools and Setup

3.1 Required Tools

1. **Go Programming Language:**
   You need to have Go installed on your machine. You can download it from the official Go website.

2. **Text Editor or IDE:**
   You can use any text editor to write Go code, but it is highly recommended to use one with Go support, such as:

   o **Visual Studio Code** with the Go extension

   o **GoLand** for a full-featured Go IDE

   o **Sublime Text** with Go support

3. **Command Line Interface (CLI):**
   A terminal or command prompt is required to run your Go programs.

3.2 Setting Up Go

1. **Install Go:**

   Follow the installation instructions for your platform on the Go Downloads Page.

2. **Verify Installation:**

   After installing Go, verify that it is correctly installed by running:

bash

go version

3. **Set Up Your Workspace:**

   By default, Go uses the ~/go directory (or C:\Go on Windows) for your workspace. You can set your own workspace path by modifying the GOPATH environment variable.

4. Hands-on Examples & Projects

4.1 Building a Concurrent Web Scraper

In this section, we will build a simple concurrent web scraper that fetches data from multiple web pages concurrently using goroutines and channels.

Step 1: Define the Scraper Function

```go
package main

import (
    "fmt"
    "net/http"
    "io/ioutil"
    "log"
)

func fetchURL(url string, ch chan<- string) {
    res, err := http.Get(url)
    if err != nil {
        ch <- fmt.Sprintf("Error fetching %s: %v", url, err)
        return
```

```go
    }
    defer res.Body.Close()
    body, err := ioutil.ReadAll(res.Body)
    if err != nil {
        ch <- fmt.Sprintf("Error reading body of
%s: %v", url, err)
        return
    }
    ch <- fmt.Sprintf("Fetched %s with length
%d", url, len(body))
}
```

Step 2: Concurrently Fetch Multiple URLs

Now we'll fetch multiple URLs concurrently:

```go
func main() {
    urls := []string{
        "https://golang.org",
        "https://www.google.com",
        "https://www.github.com",
    }

    ch := make(chan string)

    for _, url := range urls {
```

```go
        go fetchURL(url, ch)
    }

    for range urls {
        fmt.Println(<-ch) // Wait for results
from each goroutine
    }
}
```

Step 3: Running the Scraper

To run this program:

1. Save the code in a file named web_scraper.go.

2. Open your terminal and navigate to the directory containing the file.

3. Run the following command:

```bash
bash
```

```
go run web_scraper.go
```

This will fetch the content of the URLs concurrently and print out the results.

5. Advanced Techniques & Optimization

5.1 Managing Goroutines Efficiently

While goroutines are lightweight, managing too many of them can lead to performance issues. Use worker pools or limit the number of active goroutines to avoid resource exhaustion.

5.2 Optimizing Channel Usage

Avoid blocking channels and optimize their capacity by adjusting the buffer size. Buffering channels can reduce blocking and improve performance, especially when there's a high volume of data being sent between goroutines.

---

6. Troubleshooting and Problem-Solving

6.1 Common Challenges

- **Deadlocks:** Ensure that channels are being used properly and that all goroutines eventually complete.

- **Race Conditions:** Use channels and other synchronization methods (like sync.Mutex) to avoid simultaneous data access.

6.2 Debugging Tips

- **Use fmt.Println Statements:** Debugging concurrent programs can be challenging. Use print statements to trace goroutines' execution and identify issues.

- **Go Debugger (Delve):** Use Delve for step-through debugging, setting breakpoints, and inspecting the state of goroutines.

---

7. Conclusion & Next Steps

In this chapter, we've covered the fundamentals of concurrency in Go, including:

- **Goroutines:** Lightweight threads of execution that allow concurrent tasks.

- **Channels:** Safe communication mechanisms for sharing data between goroutines.

- **Best Practices:** Tips for avoiding common pitfalls like deadlocks and race conditions.

- **Hands-on Project:** We built a concurrent web scraper to demonstrate how to apply these concepts in a practical project.

Next Steps:

- **Explore More Concurrency Patterns:** Learn about advanced concurrency patterns such as worker pools and fan-out/fan-in.

- **Read More About Go's Concurrency Primitives:** Explore other synchronization mechanisms in Go like sync.Mutex and sync.WaitGroup.

With this knowledge, you are now ready to build efficient, scalable concurrent applications in Go! Happy coding!

Chapter 8: Working with Packages and the Go Ecosystem

1. Introduction

Go, also known as Golang, is a modern programming language designed by Google that emphasizes simplicity, performance, and scalability. One of the most powerful features of Go is its rich ecosystem of packages and modules, which allows developers to build applications efficiently by reusing code. Understanding how to work with Go packages and manage dependencies is crucial for building robust and maintainable Go applications. Whether you're building a web service, a CLI tool, or a data-processing pipeline, Go's package system will be a central part of your development process.

In this chapter, we will explore:

- **Go modules** and package management, explaining how to manage dependencies and versioning effectively.

- **The Go standard library**, which provides a wide range of built-in packages for everything from web servers to cryptography, making Go a versatile language for many use cases.

- **Third-party packages** and how to integrate community-driven libraries into your projects.

- **Hands-on example**: We'll build a simple REST API using popular Go libraries, demonstrating how to work with packages and third-party dependencies in practice.

By the end of this chapter, you will have a solid understanding of how to navigate Go's ecosystem and leverage the power of modules, libraries, and third-party packages in your own projects.

Why Working with Packages and the Go Ecosystem Matters

Go's ecosystem is robust, with thousands of packages available for use in various domains, including networking, web development, testing, and more. The ability to integrate these packages seamlessly into your projects can save time, reduce boilerplate, and help you focus on building core functionality rather than reinventing the wheel.

Moreover, the Go modules system introduced in Go 1.11 simplifies dependency management, allowing you to handle versions and dependencies with ease, making it much more convenient for modern software development.

In this chapter, we'll explore Go's ecosystem and how to make the most of the available tools and packages to streamline your development process. We'll also see how to efficiently manage packages with modules to avoid versioning issues and maintain a clean project setup.

---

2. Core Concepts and Theory

2.1 Go Modules and Package Management

Go modules are the primary way to manage dependencies and versioning in modern Go applications. The Go module system, introduced in Go 1.11, simplifies dependency management by making it easy to define, update, and track dependencies.

2.1.1 What are Go Modules?

A Go module is a collection of Go packages that are versioned together. Modules help you manage project dependencies and their versions in a systematic way. Before modules, Go used the GOPATH system, which was cumbersome for managing dependencies across different projects. With Go modules, each project can have its own set of dependencies, independent of the global workspace.

A Go module is defined by a go.mod file, which contains metadata about the module, such as its dependencies and the version of Go it is compatible with.

2.1.2 Creating a Go Module

To start using Go modules in your project, you need to initialize a module in the root of your project directory:

```
bash
```

```
go mod init myproject
```

This command creates a go.mod file in your project's root directory. The go.mod file keeps track of the modules your project depends on, as well as the versions of those modules.

Here's an example of what a go.mod file might look like:

```
go
```

```
module myproject

go 1.16

require (
    github.com/gin-gonic/gin v1.7.4
    github.com/jinzhu/gorm v1.9.16
)
```

The go mod init command also automatically adds the necessary dependencies, and when you run the project, Go fetches these dependencies if they're not already present in the go.mod file.

2.1.3 Managing Dependencies with Go Modules

To add a new dependency to your project, you can use the go get command. For example, to add the popular web framework **Gin**:

```bash
```

```
go get github.com/gin-gonic/gin
```
This command updates the go.mod file with the new dependency and its version, and it downloads the package.

You can also use go get to upgrade or downgrade dependencies. For example, to upgrade Gin to the latest version, you can run:

```bash

go get github.com/gin-gonic/gin@latest
```

2.1.4 The go.sum File

In addition to the go.mod file, Go also creates a go.sum file, which contains cryptographic hashes of the dependencies. This file ensures that the dependencies you download are exactly the same as the ones that were used in your project previously, preventing potential issues with tampered or corrupted dependencies.

2.2 Using the Standard Library Effectively

Go comes with an extensive standard library that covers almost every area of development. From handling HTTP requests to manipulating files and working with databases, Go's standard library provides all the tools you need to build powerful applications without relying on third-party libraries.

2.2.1 Commonly Used Packages in the Go Standard Library

Some of the most commonly used packages in Go's standard library include:

- **net/http**: Provides HTTP client and server functionality, perfect for building web services.

- **fmt**: Supports formatted I/O, similar to printf-style formatting in other languages.

- **os**: Provides functions for interacting with the operating system, including file operations, environment variables, and more.

- **encoding/json**: Used for encoding and decoding JSON data, a common format for APIs.

- **time**: Provides functionality for working with dates and times.

- **io/ioutil**: Used for reading and writing files, useful for simple file I/O operations.

2.2.2 Example: Creating a Simple Web Server with net/http

One of the most common use cases for Go is building web applications or APIs. Here's a simple example of how to create a web server using the net/http package:

```go
package main

import (
    "fmt"
    "net/http"
)

func handler(w http.ResponseWriter, r *http.Request) {
    fmt.Fprintf(w, "Hello, World!")
}

func main() {
    http.HandleFunc("/", handler)
    fmt.Println("Starting server on :8080...")
    http.ListenAndServe(":8080", nil)
}
```

In this example:

- We define a simple handler function that responds with "Hello, World!" when accessed.

- The http.HandleFunc function registers the handler to the root URL ("/").

- http.ListenAndServe starts the web server on port 8080.

2.2.3 Handling JSON Requests with encoding/json

Another important package is encoding/json, which makes it easy to parse and generate JSON data. For example, here's how to build a simple API endpoint that handles JSON data:

```go
package main

import (
    "encoding/json"
    "fmt"
    "net/http"
)

type User struct {
    Name  string `json:"name"`
    Email string `json:"email"`
```

```go
}

func userHandler(w http.ResponseWriter, r
*http.Request) {
    if r.Method == http.MethodPost {
        var user User
        decoder := json.NewDecoder(r.Body)
        if err := decoder.Decode(&user); err !=
nil {
            http.Error(w, err.Error(),
http.StatusBadRequest)
            return
        }
        fmt.Fprintf(w, "Received user: %s, %s",
user.Name, user.Email)
    } else {
        http.Error(w, "Invalid method",
http.StatusMethodNotAllowed)
    }
}

func main() {
    http.HandleFunc("/user", userHandler)
    http.ListenAndServe(":8080", nil)
}
```

In this example, we:

- Define a User struct with JSON tags to specify how fields should be serialized.

- Use json.NewDecoder to decode JSON from the HTTP request body.

- Return a response confirming the user data received.

2.3 Third-Party Packages and Community-Driven Projects

While Go's standard library is vast and covers many use cases, third-party packages play an important role in extending Go's functionality. There are numerous open-source packages available for Go, created by the community to solve common problems that Go's standard library might not address out-of-the-box.

2.3.1 Finding and Installing Third-Party Packages

To install third-party packages, you simply use the go get command:

```bash
go get github.com/gorilla/mux
```

This installs the **Gorilla Mux** package, which is a powerful HTTP router and URL matcher. Once installed, you can use the package in your Go code:

```go

package main

import (
    "fmt"
    "github.com/gorilla/mux"
    "net/http"
)

func main() {
    r := mux.NewRouter()
    r.HandleFunc("/", func(w http.ResponseWriter, r *http.Request) {
        fmt.Fprintln(w, "Hello from Gorilla Mux!")
    })
    http.ListenAndServe(":8080", r)
}
```

In this example, we use Gorilla Mux to handle HTTP routes and requests. The router is more flexible than the built-in http.HandleFunc, allowing you to match complex URL patterns.

2.3.2 Popular Third-Party Packages in Go

Some of the most popular third-party packages in Go include:

- **Gorilla Mux**: A powerful URL router and dispatcher for Go web servers.

- **Gin**: A fast web framework for building APIs, known for its performance and simplicity.

- **Gorm**: An Object Relational Mapper (ORM) for Go, making it easier to interact with databases.

- **Go-redis**: A Redis client for Go, used for connecting and interacting with Redis databases.

- **Logrus**: A structured logger for Go, often used in production environments for logging.

3. Tools and Setup

3.1 Required Tools

1. **Go Programming Language**: Download and install Go from Go's official website.

2. **Text Editor or IDE**: Use any text editor that supports Go. The recommended options are:

   o **Visual Studio Code (VS Code)** with the Go extension.

   o **GoLand**, a dedicated Go IDE.

   o **Sublime Text** with Go support.

3. **Command Line Interface (CLI)**: A terminal (macOS/Linux) or Command Prompt (Windows) is required to run your Go code.

3.2 Setting Up Go

1. **Install Go**: Follow the installation instructions on the Go Downloads Page.

2. **Verify Installation**: Run go version to verify that Go is installed correctly.

3. **Set Up Your Workspace**: Go uses the $GOPATH environment variable for workspace management. For simplicity, Go now defaults to using Go modules, so no need to set up a workspace unless you're using legacy projects.

---

4. Hands-on Examples & Projects

4.1 Creating a REST API with Popular Go Libraries

Now that we've covered the theory and the tools, let's create a REST API using Go's standard library and third-party packages. This API will manage user data, allowing us to add, retrieve, and update users.

Step 1: Set Up the Project

Initialize the project and create the go.mod file:

```bash

go mod init myrestapi
```

Step 2: Install Dependencies

Install the required dependencies for handling HTTP requests and routing:

```bash
```

```
go get github.com/gin-gonic/gin
```

Step 3: Define the User Struct

Create a User struct to represent user data:

```go
```

```
package main

import "github.com/gin-gonic/gin"

type User struct {
    ID      int     `json:"id"`
    Name    string  `json:"name"`
    Email   string  `json:"email"`
}
```

Step 4: Create the Handlers

Now, let's create handlers to get, post, and update users:

```go
```

```
var users = []User{
```

```go
    {ID: 1, Name: "John Doe", Email:
"john.doe@example.com"},
}


func getUsers(c *gin.Context) {
    c.JSON(200, users)
}


func createUser(c *gin.Context) {
    var newUser User
    if err := c.ShouldBindJSON(&newUser); err !=
nil {
        c.JSON(400, gin.H{"error": err.Error()})
        return
    }
    users = append(users, newUser)
    c.JSON(201, newUser)
}
```

Step 5: Set Up the Router and Start the Server

Now, let's set up the Gin router and start the server:

```go
go


func main() {
    r := gin.Default()
    r.GET("/users", getUsers)
```

```
    r.POST("/users", createUser)
    r.Run(":8080") // Start server on port 8080
}
```

Step 6: Test the API

Run the API server:

bash

```
go run main.go
```

You can test the endpoints using a tool like **Postman** or curl:

- To get all users:

bash

```
curl http://localhost:8080/users
```

- To create a new user:

bash

```
curl -X POST -H "Content-Type: application/json"
-d '{"id": 2, "name": "Jane Doe", "email":
"jane.doe@example.com"}'
http://localhost:8080/users
```

5. Advanced Techniques & Optimization

5.1 Optimizing Go REST APIs

- **Graceful Shutdowns**: Use http.Server with proper shutdown handling to ensure that active requests complete before the server shuts down.

- **Caching**: Implement caching with Redis or in-memory caching to reduce response times for frequently requested data.

---

6. Troubleshooting and Problem-Solving

6.1 Common Challenges

- **Versioning Issues**: Ensure that dependencies are compatible by using go mod tidy to clean up unused dependencies and update versions.

6.2 Debugging Tips

- **Check the go.mod File**: Verify that your dependencies are correctly listed in go.mod and that no incompatible versions are present.

- **Use Logs**: Use structured logging (e.g., with Logrus) to debug API requests and responses.

---

7. Conclusion & Next Steps

In this chapter, we have covered:

- How to create and manage Go modules.

- The vast Go standard library, and how to leverage it for common tasks.

- How to integrate third-party libraries into your projects.

- A hands-on example of creating a simple REST API using popular Go libraries.

Next Steps:

- **Explore More Go Libraries**: Go has an ever-growing ecosystem of third-party libraries for different domains. Explore libraries like Gorm for ORM, Go-redis for Redis, or Go-graphql for building GraphQL APIs.

- **Build More APIs**: Continue building APIs using Go, incorporating advanced concepts like authentication, middleware, and logging.

With Go's package system and its rich ecosystem, you now have the tools to build powerful, maintainable applications. Happy coding!

Chapter 9: Testing, Debugging, and Optimizing Go Code

1. Introduction

Writing efficient, maintainable, and bug-free code is a goal every developer strives for. In Go, testing, debugging, and optimization are integral parts of the software development lifecycle. Whether you're working on a small script or a large-scale application, ensuring that your code works as expected and performs efficiently is key to building reliable software.

In this chapter, we'll explore Go's approach to **testing**, **debugging**, and **optimization**. We'll cover:

- **Writing tests in Go**: Understanding how to write unit tests and integration tests to ensure your code behaves as expected.

- **Debugging techniques and tools**: Exploring how to debug Go code and identify issues efficiently using various tools.

- **Performance optimization and profiling**: Learning how to analyze and optimize the performance of your Go applications.

We'll also walk through a hands-on example of **test-driven development (TDD)**, refactoring a project by writing tests first and then iterating to improve the code. By the end of this chapter, you'll be equipped with the skills to write efficient and maintainable Go applications, backed by solid testing practices and optimized for performance.

Why Testing, Debugging, and Optimization Matter

Testing, debugging, and optimization are crucial for building production-ready Go applications. Here's why they matter:

- **Testing** ensures that your code behaves as expected and can handle edge cases, giving you confidence that changes won't introduce new bugs.

- **Debugging** helps you identify and fix issues, making it easier to track down problems when something goes wrong.

- **Optimization** improves the performance of your code, ensuring that it runs efficiently even as your application scales.

By mastering these three areas, you can improve the quality, reliability, and performance of your Go applications.

---

2. Core Concepts and Theory

2.1 Writing Tests in Go

Testing is essential for writing reliable software. Go has a built-in testing framework that makes it easy to write and run tests. These tests help ensure that your code functions as expected and can be safely refactored or extended.

2.1.1 Unit Tests

A **unit test** tests a single function or unit of code in isolation. The goal is to verify that each part of your program works as expected under various conditions. In Go, unit tests are written in files ending with _test.go and use the testing package to define test functions.

Example: Writing a Unit Test

Let's write a simple unit test for a function that adds two integers:

```go
package main

import "testing"

// Function to be tested
func Add(a, b int) int {
    return a + b
}

// Unit test for Add function
func TestAdd(t *testing.T) {
    result := Add(2, 3)
    expected := 5
    if result != expected {
        t.Errorf("Add(2, 3) = %d; expected %d",
result, expected)
    }
```

}

In this example:

- We define the Add function, which simply adds two integers.

- The TestAdd function is a test function, defined with the signature TestXxx(t *testing.T), where Xxx is the name of the function being tested.

- If the test fails, t.Errorf is called to log an error message.

Running the Test

To run the tests, use the go test command in the terminal:

bash

go test

If the test passes, you'll see an output like:

bash

PASS
ok   example 0.002s

If the test fails, Go will show an error message indicating where the test failed.

2.1.2 Test Coverage

Test coverage refers to the percentage of code covered by tests. While 100% coverage is not always necessary, having high test coverage can help ensure that your code is reliable.

Go provides a built-in tool to measure test coverage. To run tests with coverage information:

```bash
```

```bash
go test -cover
```
The output will show the percentage of your code that is covered by tests.

2.1.3 Integration Tests

Integration tests test how multiple components of your application work together. These tests often interact with external systems, such as databases or web services.

Example: Writing an Integration Test

Let's write an integration test for a function that interacts with an external API (e.g., fetching a user's data):

```go
```

```go
package main
```

```go
import (
    "net/http"
    "testing"
)

func FetchUserData(url string) (*http.Response,
error) {
    return http.Get(url)
}

func TestFetchUserData(t *testing.T) {
    url :=
"https://jsonplaceholder.typicode.com/users/1"
    response, err := FetchUserData(url)
    if err != nil {
        t.Errorf("Failed to fetch data: %v", err)
    }
    if response.StatusCode != 200 {
        t.Errorf("Expected status code 200; got
%d", response.StatusCode)
    }
}
```

In this example, the FetchUserData function makes a request
to an external API. The TestFetchUserData test checks if the
API returns a status code of 200.

2.2 Debugging Techniques and Tools

Debugging is an essential skill for identifying and fixing issues in your code. Go provides a range of tools and techniques for debugging, making it easier to track down problems.

2.2.1 Print-Based Debugging

The simplest form of debugging is using fmt.Println to print variables and inspect the state of your program. This method is useful for quick checks or simple bugs, but it's not ideal for complex debugging tasks.

```go
```

```go
fmt.Println("Debugging value of x:", x)
```

2.2.2 The Go Debugger (Delve)

For more complex debugging tasks, Go provides **Delve**, a powerful debugger that allows you to set breakpoints, inspect variables, and step through your code. To install Delve:

```bash
```

```bash
go get -u github.com/go-delve/delve/cmd/dlv
```

To start debugging with Delve:

```bash
```

```
dlv debug
```

This launches the debugger and allows you to set breakpoints, examine variables, and step through the program interactively.

2.2.3 Logging

For ongoing debugging in production environments, structured logging is a best practice. Go's standard library includes the log package, but for more advanced features, you can use third-party libraries like **Logrus** or **Zap** for structured and leveled logging.

```go
import "github.com/sirupsen/logrus"

log := logrus.New()
log.Info("This is an info log")
log.Error("This is an error log")
```

2.2.4 Panic and Recover

Go's panic and recover mechanisms are useful for handling unexpected errors. A panic causes the program to stop, but you can use recover within a deferred function to recover from a panic and resume execution.

```go
go

func mayPanic() {
    panic("Something went wrong!")
}

func safeFunction() {
    defer func() {
        if r := recover(); r != nil {
            fmt.Println("Recovered from panic:",
r)
        }
    }()
    mayPanic()
}
```

In this example, safeFunction handles the panic gracefully, allowing the program to continue.

2.3 Performance Optimization and Profiling

Optimizing the performance of your Go code is crucial, especially for high-performance applications. Go provides a range of tools to measure and optimize the performance of your programs.

2.3.1 Profiling with pprof

Go includes the net/http/pprof package, which provides runtime profiling for CPU and memory usage. To enable profiling, import the pprof package and start an HTTP server:

```go
go

import (
    _ "net/http/pprof"
    "net/http"
    "log"
)

func main() {
    go func() {

log.Println(http.ListenAndServe("localhost:6060",
nil))
    }()
}
```

With the profiling server running, you can visit http://localhost:6060/debug/pprof/ to view various profiles, such as CPU, heap, and goroutine statistics.

2.3.2 Benchmarking

Go has built-in support for benchmarking through the testing package. You can create benchmarks to measure the performance of functions.

Example: Writing a Benchmark

```go
go
```

```go
func BenchmarkAdd(b *testing.B) {
    for i := 0; i < b.N; i++ {
        Add(2, 3)
    }
}
```

To run benchmarks, use the go test command with the -bench flag:

```bash
bash
```

```bash
go test -bench .
```

This will run the benchmark and show you the performance of the Add function in terms of time taken per operation.

2.3.3 Memory Optimization

Memory optimization is crucial for applications that need to scale or handle large amounts of data. Some strategies include:

- **Avoiding Memory Leaks**: Use defer to close resources like files and database connections to prevent memory leaks.

- **Using Value Types Wisely**: When working with large structs, consider passing pointers instead of values to avoid unnecessary ing.

2.3.4 Identifying Hotspots

You can use Go's profiling tools to identify bottlenecks in your code. Once you have identified slow functions, focus on optimizing them by reducing complexity or using more efficient algorithms.

3. Tools and Setup

3.1 Required Tools

- **Go programming language**: Install Go from Go's official website.

- **Text Editor or IDE**: Use an editor like **Visual Studio Code** (with Go extension) or **GoLand** for an integrated experience.

- **Go Testing Tools**: Go's built-in testing package for writing tests.

- **Delve**: A debugger for Go. Install it with:

```bash
go get -u github.com/go-delve/delve/cmd/dlv
```

- **pprof**: Built-in package for runtime profiling in Go.

---

4. Hands-on Examples & Projects

4.1 Refactoring a Project with Test-Driven Development (TDD)

In this section, we will refactor a simple project using TDD. We will start by writing tests, then refactor the code to make it pass the tests.

Step 1: Write a Failing Test

Let's say we have a simple function that calculates the factorial of a number. We'll start by writing a test for it:

```go
package main
```

```go
import "testing"

func TestFactorial(t *testing.T) {
    result := Factorial(5)
    expected := 120
    if result != expected {
        t.Errorf("Factorial(5) = %d; expected
%d", result, expected)
    }
}
```

Step 2: Write the Function to Pass the Test

Now, we implement the Factorial function to make the test pass:

```go
go

func Factorial(n int) int {
    if n == 0 {
        return 1
    }
    return n * Factorial(n-1)
}
```

Step 3: Refactor and Add More Tests

After passing the test, we refactor the code to improve its performance or readability and add additional test cases to cover edge cases.

---

5. Advanced Techniques & Optimization

5.1 Optimizing Tests for Speed

As your project grows, you might find that running tests takes longer. To speed up your tests, consider:

- **Parallelizing Tests**: Use the t.Parallel() method to run tests concurrently.

- **Mocking External Services**: Use mocking libraries like **GoMock** or **Testify** to simulate external services during tests.

---

6. Troubleshooting and Problem-Solving

6.1 Common Challenges

- **Flaky Tests:** Tests that intermittently fail can be challenging. To address this, ensure that your tests are independent and avoid relying on external state.

- **Slow Tests:** Optimize tests by minimizing external dependencies, using mock services, and avoiding unnecessary complexity in tests.

6.2 Debugging Tips

- **Use log.Printf for detailed output** during development to track the state of variables.

- **Use Delve** to step through code and analyze the stack traces when debugging complex issues.

---

7. Conclusion & Next Steps

In this chapter, we've explored:

- Writing **unit** and **integration tests** in Go.

- Using debugging tools like **Delve** and the **Go pprof** package.

- Techniques for **performance optimization** and **profiling.**

Next Steps:

- Continue practicing **test-driven development (TDD)** by refactoring more complex projects.

- Explore **advanced debugging** and **profiling** techniques to analyze performance bottlenecks in larger applications.

By mastering testing, debugging, and optimization, you will be able to write more reliable, performant, and maintainable Go applications. Happy coding!

Chapter 10: Real-World Applications and Advanced Topics

1. Introduction

Go (Golang) has quickly become one of the most popular programming languages for building scalable, high-performance applications. Its simplicity, efficiency, and ease of concurrency make it an excellent choice for real-world applications that need to handle complex systems and large-scale environments. Whether you're building a web application, integrating with cloud services, or designing a microservices architecture, Go provides a robust and reliable foundation for your projects.

In this chapter, we will delve into more advanced topics in Go, focusing on its real-world applications in enterprise software development. Specifically, we will cover:

- **Integrating Go with databases and cloud services**: Learn how to interact with databases and integrate Go applications with cloud platforms, which is a critical part of most modern applications.

- **Introduction to microservices architecture in Go**: Explore the concepts behind microservices and how to use Go to build efficient, decoupled microservices that can be easily scaled.

- **Deploying Go applications in production environments**: Understand the best practices for deploying Go applications, from containerization with Docker to cloud-based deployments on platforms like AWS, GCP, or Azure.

- **Hands-on**: We will develop a **microservice** for a logistics platform, demonstrating how to apply the principles and tools we've discussed in the chapter.

By the end of this chapter, you will have a solid understanding of how to integrate Go with databases, leverage microservices architecture, and deploy Go applications to production environments. You'll be ready to tackle real-world projects that require scalability, performance, and reliability.

Why Real-World Applications and Advanced Topics Matter

As Go continues to gain popularity, it has been adopted by many companies for large-scale systems due to its ability to efficiently handle concurrent tasks and its lightweight execution. Building real-world applications in Go involves more than just writing clean and effective code. It requires an understanding of integration with external systems, scalability through microservices, and deploying your applications in cloud environments.

These advanced topics help you become proficient in creating applications that can handle high traffic, data storage, and deployment challenges, making Go a valuable tool for modern enterprise development.

---

2. Core Concepts and Theory

2.1 Integrating Go with Databases and Cloud Services

In modern software development, applications often rely on databases to store and retrieve data, while cloud services offer the infrastructure and scalability needed to deploy applications effectively. Integrating Go with these technologies allows you to build systems that can scale, perform, and maintain high availability.

2.1.1 Go and Databases

Go supports integration with various relational and NoSQL databases through both the standard library and third-party packages. The most common database integrations are with **SQL databases** (such as MySQL, PostgreSQL) and **NoSQL databases** (like MongoDB, Redis).

Example: Connecting Go to a PostgreSQL Database

One of the most popular relational databases is PostgreSQL. To connect Go to PostgreSQL, you can use the pq driver.

1. **Install the pq Driver:**

```bash
go get github.com/lib/pq
```

2. **Code to Connect to PostgreSQL:**

```go
```

```go
package main

import (
    "database/sql"
    "fmt"
    "log"

    _ "github.com/lib/pq"
)

func main() {
    connStr := "user=username dbname=mydb sslmode=disable"
    db, err := sql.Open("postgres", connStr)
    if err != nil {
        log.Fatal(err)
    }
    defer db.Close()

    rows, err := db.Query("SELECT id, name FROM users")
    if err != nil {
        log.Fatal(err)
    }
    defer rows.Close()
```

```
for rows.Next() {
    var id int
    var name string
    if err := rows.Scan(&id, &name); err !=
nil {
        log.Fatal(err)
    }
    fmt.Println(id, name)
}
}
```

In this example:

- We connect to a PostgreSQL database using the pq driver.

- We query the users table and print out the id and name fields.

2.1.2 Go and Cloud Services

Go is a great fit for cloud-based applications due to its speed, efficiency, and scalability. Cloud services like **AWS, Google Cloud Platform (GCP)**, and **Microsoft Azure** offer APIs that can be integrated into Go applications for a variety of use cases, including storage, compute, messaging, and machine learning.

Example: Interfacing with AWS S3

To interact with AWS S3 (Simple Storage Service) in Go, you need the **AWS SDK for Go.** Install it by running:

```bash
go get github.com/aws/aws-sdk-go
```

Then, you can upload and download files to and from S3 as follows:

```go
package main

import (
    "fmt"
    "log"

    "github.com/aws/aws-sdk-go/aws"
    "github.com/aws/aws-sdk-go/aws/session"
    "github.com/aws/aws-sdk-go/service/s3"
)

func uploadFile(bucket, key, filename string) {
    sess, err := session.NewSession(&aws.Config{
        Region: aws.String("us-west-2")},
```

```
)
if err != nil {
    log.Fatal(err)
}

svc := s3.New(sess)
file, err := os.Open(filename)
if err != nil {
    log.Fatal(err)
}
defer file.Close()

_, err = svc.PutObject(&s3.PutObjectInput{
    Bucket: aws.String(bucket),
    Key:    aws.String(key),
    Body:   file,
})
if err != nil {
    log.Fatal(err)
}

fmt.Println("File uploaded successfully.")
}
```

In this example, we use the **AWS SDK** to upload a file to an S3 bucket, which is a common use case for cloud services.

2.2 Introduction to Microservices Architecture in Go

Microservices architecture has become a popular design pattern for building scalable and maintainable software systems. In this architecture, an application is divided into small, loosely coupled services that are independently deployable and communicate over a network.

2.2.1 What is a Microservice?

A **microservice** is a small, self-contained unit that handles a specific functionality of a larger system. Each service has its own database and communicates with other services using lightweight protocols like HTTP, gRPC, or message queues.

Example: Benefits of Microservices

- **Scalability**: Each service can be scaled independently based on its specific load.

- **Resilience**: If one microservice fails, others can continue to function, making the system more robust.

- **Flexibility:** Microservices can be developed and deployed independently, which enables faster iteration and updates.

2.2.2 Microservices in Go

Go's simplicity, concurrency model, and performance make it an ideal language for building microservices. You can build RESTful APIs, manage inter-service communication, and ensure high availability in distributed environments.

Example: Creating a Simple Microservice in Go

Here's a simple example of a REST API microservice built with Go's **Gin** web framework:

```go
go


package main

import (
    "github.com/gin-gonic/gin"
    "net/http"
)

func main() {
    r := gin.Default()
```

```
r.GET("/products", func(c *gin.Context) {
    c.JSON(http.StatusOK, gin.H{
        "products": []string{"Product1",
"Product2", "Product3"},
    })
})

r.Run(":8080")
}
```

In this example, we create a microservice with the following features:

- **GET /products** endpoint returns a list of products.

- The microservice is independent and could be deployed in isolation, while other services in the system might handle users, orders, or inventory.

2.3 Deploying Go Applications in Production Environments

Deploying Go applications into production involves a series of steps that ensure the application is reliable, scalable, and maintainable in a live environment. This typically involves packaging the application into a Docker container, managing the deployment, and setting up monitoring and scaling.

2.3.1 Containerizing Go Applications with Docker

One of the best ways to deploy Go applications is by containerizing them using **Docker**. Docker enables you to package your application with all its dependencies into a lightweight container that can be easily deployed anywhere.

Example: Dockerizing a Go Application

1. **Dockerfile**: Create a Dockerfile in the root of your Go project:

Dockerfile

```
# Use the official Go image from Docker Hub
FROM golang:1.16-alpine as builder

WORKDIR /app

#  the Go source code
 . .

# Build the Go binary
RUN go build -o myapp .
```

```
# Final image
FROM alpine:latest

WORKDIR /root/

#  the binary from the builder image
 --from=builder /app/myapp .

# Expose port
EXPOSE 8080

# Run the application
CMD ["./myapp"]
```

2. **Build and Run Docker Image:**

```bash
bash
```

```
docker build -t my-go-app .
docker run -p 8080:8080 my-go-app
```

This creates a Docker image for the Go application and runs it inside a container.

2.3.2 Deploying to Cloud Platforms

Once you have your Go application in a container, you can deploy it to cloud platforms like **AWS**, **Google Cloud**, or

Microsoft Azure. These platforms support container orchestration tools like **Kubernetes,** which help manage the deployment, scaling, and monitoring of containerized applications.

Example: Deploying to Kubernetes

1. **Kubernetes YAML configuration:** Create a deployment.yaml file to deploy the containerized Go app:

yaml

```yaml
apiVersion: apps/v1
kind: Deployment
metadata:
  name: my-go-app
spec:
  replicas: 3
  selector:
    matchLabels:
      app: my-go-app
  template:
    metadata:
      labels:
        app: my-go-app
    spec:
```

```
containers:
- name: my-go-app
  image: my-go-app:latest
  ports:
  - containerPort: 8080
```

2. **Deploy to Kubernetes**:

```bash
bash
```

```
kubectl apply -f deployment.yaml
```

This will deploy the Go application with three replicas, ensuring high availability.

---

3. Tools and Setup

3.1 Required Tools

1. **Go Programming Language**: Install Go from Go's official website.

2. **Docker**: Install Docker from Docker's official website.

3. **Kubernetes**: Install Kubernetes and use kubectl for managing Kubernetes clusters. You can also use services like **Google Kubernetes Engine (GKE)**, **Amazon EKS**, or **Azure AKS** for managed Kubernetes.

4. **Cloud SDKs**: Install cloud SDKs like **AWS CLI**, **Google Cloud SDK**, or **Azure CLI** to interact with cloud services.

---

4. Hands-on Examples & Projects

4.1 Developing a Microservice for a Logistics Platform

In this section, we will build a simple microservice for a logistics platform that manages delivery information.

Step 1: Define the Microservice

We'll create a Delivery struct to represent a delivery, and we'll build **API** endpoints to manage deliveries.

```go
package main

import (
    "github.com/gin-gonic/gin"
    "net/http"
)
```

```go
type Delivery struct {
    ID       string `json:"id"`
    Address  string `json:"address"`
    Status   string `json:"status"`
}


var deliveries = []Delivery{
    {ID: "1", Address: "123 Main St", Status: "In
Transit"},
    {ID: "2", Address: "456 Elm St", Status:
"Delivered"},
}


func getDeliveries(c *gin.Context) {
    c.JSON(http.StatusOK, deliveries)
}


func main() {
    r := gin.Default()
    r.GET("/deliveries", getDeliveries)
    r.Run(":8080")
}
```

This microservice has an endpoint that returns the list of deliveries.

Step 2: Containerize the Application

Follow the Dockerfile steps mentioned earlier to package the Go application.

Step 3: Deploy the Microservice

- Deploy the microservice to a cloud service or a Kubernetes cluster.

- Use Kubernetes to scale and manage the service in a production environment.

---

5. Advanced Techniques & Optimization

5.1 Scaling Microservices with Kubernetes

Kubernetes allows you to scale microservices horizontally by increasing the number of replicas. For example, you can configure Kubernetes to scale the **Delivery Service** based on traffic patterns.

5.2 Load Balancing and Auto-scaling

Set up **Horizontal Pod Autoscaling (HPA)** in Kubernetes to automatically adjust the number of replicas based on CPU utilization or other metrics.

---

6. Troubleshooting and Problem-Solving

6.1 Common Challenges

- **Service Communication:** Microservices often need to communicate with each other. Use **gRPC** or **RESTful APIs** to handle this communication.

- **Database Integration:** Managing databases across microservices can be complex. Use **database per service** pattern or **shared databases** carefully.

6.2 Debugging Tips

- **Use Distributed Tracing:** Tools like **Jaeger** or **Zipkin** help trace requests across microservices.

- **Check Logs:** Centralize logs using services like **Elasticsearch, Kibana,** or **Grafana** to make debugging easier.

---

7. Conclusion & Next Steps

In this chapter, we covered:

- Integrating Go with databases and cloud services.

- Understanding and building microservices using Go.

- Deploying Go applications in production environments.

Next Steps:

- Experiment with more complex microservices.

- Explore advanced **Kubernetes** and **cloud services** for managing large-scale Go applications.

- Learn about **event-driven architectures** and **message queues** like **RabbitMQ** or **Kafka** for handling asynchronous operations in distributed systems.

With this knowledge, you are ready to build robust, scalable applications using Go in real-world environments. Happy coding!

Chapter 11: Project Showcase: Bringing It All Together

1. Introduction

Throughout this book, we've covered a wide range of topics that collectively provide you with the knowledge to build, optimize, and deploy applications using Go. From the basics of syntax to advanced topics like microservices and performance optimization, you now have the foundational skills required to tackle real-world problems using Go.

In this chapter, we will tie all these concepts together in a **comprehensive project**. This project will span multiple chapters, involving everything from planning and coding to testing, debugging, and deploying a fully-functional Go application. We'll work through each phase step by step, offering detailed instructions on how to structure, build, and deliver an application that adheres to best practices.

Why This Project Matters

This project is an opportunity to take the skills you've learned and apply them in a meaningful, practical way. By combining different aspects of Go—from structuring code and working with databases to optimizing performance and deploying to production—you'll gain invaluable hands-on experience that will be applicable in any real-world scenario.

Furthermore, this chapter will guide you through common troubleshooting and optimization techniques, giving you the tools to address challenges and improve your application as it evolves.

Key Concepts and Terminology

Before diving into the project, let's refresh on the key concepts and tools you'll need to complete this hands-on exercise:

- **Go Modules**: For managing project dependencies.

- **Microservices**: Small, self-contained services that interact with each other.

- **Testing and Debugging**: Methods for ensuring your application works as expected and troubleshooting issues.

- **Cloud Services**: Platforms that provide resources and services to deploy, store, and scale applications.

- **Docker and Kubernetes**: Tools for containerizing and orchestrating application deployments.

The project will integrate all these concepts and provide a complete pipeline from local development to cloud deployment. Let's begin!

---

2. Core Concepts and Theory

2.1 Understanding the Project

Our goal is to build a **logistics platform** as a microservice-based application. The application will handle basic logistics tasks such as managing deliveries and tracking shipments. It will be built with Go, leveraging databases, cloud services, and containerization to ensure scalability and performance.

The key components of the system will include:

- **Delivery Management Service**: A service to handle all the delivery operations.

- **Inventory Service:** A service for managing inventory, tied to the delivery service.

- **API Gateway:** An entry point for all requests, directing them to the appropriate microservice.

- **Database Integration:** Using PostgreSQL to store data and ensure data consistency across services.

- **Cloud Deployment:** Deploying the system to a cloud service (e.g., AWS, GCP).

2.1.1 Microservices Architecture

Microservices allow different parts of the system to scale independently. Each service will be built and deployed separately, which provides flexibility and allows individual services to be updated or scaled without affecting the rest of the application.

Each microservice will:

- Be responsible for a specific domain (e.g., inventory, delivery).

- Communicate with other services through HTTP APIs.

- Have its own database to ensure loose coupling.

We'll be building the **Delivery Management Service** and **Inventory Service** first, followed by integrating these services through APIs.

2.1.2 Structuring the Project

A well-structured project is essential for scalability and maintainability. Here's how we'll organize our Go project:

- **cmd**: This directory will contain the main application entry points, such as the API gateway.

- **internal**: This will contain the core business logic, including service definitions, models, and database interactions.

- **pkg**: Reusable packages and utilities (e.g., error handling, common middleware).

- **deploy**: Kubernetes configurations, Dockerfiles, and deployment scripts.

- **scripts**: Helper scripts for development and testing.

2.2 Testing, Debugging, and Optimizing the Application

Before we start writing code, it's essential to have a plan for testing and debugging the application:

- **Unit Testing:** Test individual components, such as database interactions or delivery service logic.

- **Integration Testing:** Ensure that the services work together as expected. For example, testing the communication between the delivery and inventory services.

- **Debugging:** Using Go's built-in debugging tools (e.g., delve) to identify and fix issues during development.

- **Optimization:** Once the application is functional, we'll profile it using Go's pprof tool to find bottlenecks and improve performance.

3. Tools and Setup

3.1 Required Tools

To build and deploy this project, you'll need the following tools:

1. **Go Programming Language**: Download Go from Go's official website.

2. **PostgreSQL**: Install PostgreSQL locally or use a managed instance in the cloud.

3. **Docker**: For containerizing the application.

4. **Kubernetes (optional)**: For orchestrating the deployment of services (use a local cluster like Minikube or a managed service like GKE or EKS).

5. **Git**: For version control and collaboration.

6. **Go Modules**: For managing project dependencies.

3.2 Setting Up the Development Environment

1. **Install Go**: Follow the installation instructions for your operating system from the official Go website.

2. **PostgreSQL Setup**:

- o Install PostgreSQL locally or use a cloud service like **AWS RDS** or **Google Cloud SQL**.

- o Create a database for the logistics platform.

3. **Docker Setup:**

- o Install Docker from Docker's website.

- o Verify Docker installation by running docker -- version in the terminal.

4. **Kubernetes Setup** (Optional for production deployment):

- o Install **Minikube** or use a cloud-managed Kubernetes service.

Once your environment is set up, you're ready to start coding and building the logistics platform.

---

4. Hands-on Examples & Projects

4.1 Step-by-Step: Building the Logistics Platform

Let's break down the project into smaller, manageable tasks.

4.1.1 Step 1: Create the Delivery Management Service

First, let's write the core business logic for handling deliveries. This service will expose REST endpoints for creating and retrieving deliveries.

1. **Define the Delivery Model:**

```go
package models

type Delivery struct {
    ID          string `json:"id"`
    Address     string `json:"address"`
    Status      string `json:"status"`
    DeliveredAt string
`json:"delivered_at,omitempty"`
}
```

2. **Define the Delivery Service:**

```go
package service

import (
    "log"
```

```go
    "github.com/yourusername/logistics/models"
)


var deliveries = []models.Delivery{
    {ID: "1", Address: "123 Main St", Status: "In Transit"},
    {ID: "2", Address: "456 Elm St", Status: "Delivered"},
}


func GetAllDeliveries() []models.Delivery {
    return deliveries
}


func CreateDelivery(d models.Delivery) {
    deliveries = append(deliveries, d)
    log.Println("Created new delivery:", d)
}
```

4.1.2 Step 2: Create the API Gateway

We'll use **Gin** for routing and handling HTTP requests.

1. **Define Routes:**

```go
package main
```

```go
import (
    "github.com/gin-gonic/gin"
    "github.com/yourusername/logistics/service"
    "github.com/yourusername/logistics/models"
)

func main() {
    r := gin.Default()

    r.GET("/deliveries", func(c *gin.Context) {
        deliveries := service.GetAllDeliveries()
        c.JSON(200, deliveries)
    })

    r.POST("/deliveries", func(c *gin.Context) {
        var newDelivery models.Delivery
        if err := c.ShouldBindJSON(&newDelivery);
err != nil {
            c.JSON(400, gin.H{"error":
err.Error()})
            return
        }
        service.CreateDelivery(newDelivery)
        c.JSON(201, newDelivery)
    })
```

```
r.Run(":8080")
}
```

2. **Run the Application:**

- o Run the application with go run main.go.

- o Test the API using curl or Postman.

4.1.3 Step 3: Integrate the Inventory Service

Now, let's implement a basic inventory service. This service will track items in stock, which can be used by the delivery service.

1. **Define the Inventory Model:**

go

```
package models

type Inventory struct {
    ID        string `json:"id"`
    Name      string `json:"name"`
    Quantity  int    `json:"quantity"`
}
```

2. **Define the Inventory Service:**

go

```go
package service

import (
    "log"
    "github.com/yourusername/logistics/models"
)

var inventory = []models.Inventory{
    {ID: "1", Name: "Widget", Quantity: 100},
    {ID: "2", Name: "Gadget", Quantity: 50},
}

func GetAllInventory() []models.Inventory {
    return inventory
}

func UpdateInventory(id string, qty int) {
    for i, item := range inventory {
        if item.ID == id {
            inventory[i].Quantity = qty
            log.Println("Updated inventory item:", item)
            return
        }
    }
}
```

}

4.1.4 Step 4: Test the Services

1. **Write Unit Tests**: Use Go's built-in testing package to write unit tests for each service. For example, test the GetAllDeliveries and CreateDelivery functions.

2. **Integration Testing**: Test the integration between the **Delivery Service** and **Inventory Service**. Ensure the API correctly interacts with both services.

---

5. Advanced Techniques & Optimization

5.1 Optimizing the Delivery Service

Once the application is functional, it's time to optimize it. Focus on areas like database queries, service communication, and error handling.

5.1.1 Performance Optimization

Use **Go's pprof** tool to analyze the performance of your application and identify bottlenecks.

5.1.2 Database Optimization

Consider using **database indexes** or **caching** mechanisms (like Redis) to optimize database queries and reduce response times.

---

6. Troubleshooting and Problem-Solving

6.1 Common Issues

- **Database Connectivity**: Ensure that the PostgreSQL database is running and that your Go application is correctly connected.

- **API Gateway Errors**: Double-check the routes and ensure they are correctly configured.

- **Service Communication**: When integrating multiple microservices, ensure that they can communicate effectively using REST APIs or gRPC.

6.2 Debugging Tips

- Use **Go's debugger** (Delve) to step through the code and inspect variables.

- Review **error logs** for helpful debugging information.

---

7. Conclusion & Next Steps

In this chapter, we've walked through the complete process of developing a **logistics platform** using Go. We covered:

- Planning and structuring the project.

- Building and integrating microservices.

- Testing, debugging, and deploying the application.

Next Steps:

- Explore **Kubernetes** and **Docker** further to containerize and deploy your application to the cloud.

- Learn about **message queues** (e.g., RabbitMQ, Kafka) to handle asynchronous communication between services.

- Experiment with more complex architectures like **event-driven systems.**

With this hands-on project experience, you're now equipped to tackle more advanced Go projects and continue expanding your Go expertise.